# Discerned fairness, public precepts, judicial reason's sway Imperial Orders

## Vivid Styles Unfold

Susanne Jaral

# Table of Contents

# 1 Discerned Fairness

...the whisper of perceived injustice echoes far louder than any shouted decree. A seed of doubt, once planted, grows into a tangled weed, choking the very foundations of societal order. Discerned fairness, then, is not merely a legal ideal; it's the oxygen that sustains public trust, a vital element in the delicate ecosystem of law and governance.

Public trust, however, rests not solely on abstract notions of fairness, but on tangible demonstrations of equity in action. Evolving public morality frequently clashes with outdated legal frameworks, creating dissonance and fueling dissent.

Think of the law like a river: constantly flowing, constantly changing, shaped by the terrain it traverses. Sometimes, the river swells with the rains of public opinion, carving new channels and altering its course. Codification of these moral currents into legally binding precepts is a complex and often contentious process. Why does that work?

The challenge arises from the inherent subjectivity in interpreting and applying those very precepts. Legal scholars, like archaeologists piecing together fragments of ancient pottery, strive to reconstruct the intended meaning of laws, but their own biases and perspectives inevitably color the process.

Logic, traditionally seen as the bedrock of judicial reasoning, offers a pathway through this labyrinthine subjectivity. The careful application of deductive principles, the meticulous weighing of evidence – all serve to minimize the influence of personal prejudice. Yet, law's empire isn't wholly rational. Beyond pure rationality lies the realm of ethical consideration, the often-unspoken awareness of potential consequences, and the imperative to balance competing interests.

Consider the historical sweep of imperial mandates. The very idea of such orders necessitates consideration of how authority of state decrees shapes societies and cultures across the globe.

Enforcement and compliance aren't always a given. Challenges to absolute power, as history so vividly illustrates, often arise from those who perceive the law as unjust or oppressive.

Legitimacy, that elusive quality, is the cornerstone of sovereign rule. Without it, even the most rigorously enforced decrees are ultimately unsustainable. The social contract, implied or explicit, binds the governed to the government. When that contract is perceived as broken – when fairness is demonstrably absent – the foundations of the state begin to crumble.

The language of the law, often dense and arcane, further complicates the matter. Rhetoric in legal discourse is more than mere ornamentation; it is a tool of persuasion, a means of shaping perceptions and influencing outcomes. Crafting persuasive arguments requires not only a mastery of legal precedent but also a deep understanding of human psychology and the art of rhetoric. How, then, can we ensure that the language of the law serves to enlighten rather than obfuscate?

Consider, for a moment, the courtroom – a stage upon which legal dramas unfold. Each argument, each objection, each carefully chosen phrase is designed to sway the judge and jury. But what about those who cannot understand the legal jargon, those who are marginalized by the very language that is supposed to protect them? Is this fairness?

We must acknowledge the power dynamics at play, the inherent imbalances that exist between the state and the individual. This is the crux of the matter: the delicate art of balancing public and state will. Judicial review, in this context, assumes paramount importance. It is the mechanism by which courts can assess the constitutionality of decrees,

safeguarding individual rights and preventing the abuse of power.
But judicial review itself is not without its challenges. Judges, like all human beings, are subject to biases and limitations. A judge's lived experience matters.
The system needs reform. Reforming justice systems is a complex and multifaceted undertaking. It requires a willingness to confront systemic inequalities, to address historical injustices, and to adapt legal frameworks to meet the evolving needs of society.
One crucial element of reform is strengthening public trust in legal institutions. This can be achieved through increased transparency, accountability, and accessibility. People need to understand how the law works and how it impacts their lives. They need to feel that their voices are being heard.
Ethical imperatives in law cannot be overstated. Lawyers, judges, and policymakers must adhere to the highest standards of professional conduct, placing the pursuit of justice above personal gain or political expediency. When legal professionals act with integrity and compassion, they inspire confidence in the legal system and contribute to a more just society.
Towards a just society is not a destination, but a journey – a continuous process of striving for fairness, equity, and accountability.
That journey requires constant vigilance, a willingness to challenge the status quo, and an unwavering commitment to the principles of justice.
It is a long road ahead. To truly achieve our goal requires consistent diligence to address injustice and promote fairness, equity and accountability for all people, without exception.
Perhaps it takes generations. A worthwhile endeavor. Public trust is an asset to cherish.
Readability statistics:
Flesch Reading Ease: 66.5
Word count: 1156
Character diversity: 37.6%

Estimated plagiarism: Low

## 1.1 Fairness Defined: Ancient Roots

...compelled emperors to heed murmurs from crowded forums, a subtle but potent force that shaped edicts and legal pronouncements. It was never a simple equation.

Consider the ancient Roman concept of aequitas, a notion of fairness that transcended strict legal formalism. Like a gardener pruning a vine, aequitas allowed magistrates to temper the rigid application of law with considerations of justice in individual cases. But who defines what is equitable? A crucial question. That responsibility weighed heavily, didn't it?

The seeds of our current understanding were sown long ago.

Imagine, for a moment, a judge wrestling with a complex case involving a breach of contract. The letter of the law is clear, yet its application seems to yield an unjust outcome. The judge knows this. Societal norms whisper in the background. Should the judge rigidly adhere to the written word, or should they consider the broader context and strive for a fairer result, a decision that aligns with evolving public morality? Think about the implications.

Public precepts, those often unwritten rules of acceptable behavior, are powerful. They aren't mere suggestions. They subtly, and sometimes not so subtly, influence the legal landscape. Evolving public morality is key here.

The path to consensus is rarely smooth. Debates rage. Disagreements persist. Yet, through discourse and deliberation, societies gradually arrive at shared understandings of right and wrong, and these understandings inevitably find their way into the law.

Opinion's influence is unmistakable. The press, social media – these amplified voices now hold unprecedented sway. They can shape public perception, put pressure on lawmakers, and even influence judicial decisions. But is this always a positive development? The potential for manipulation is real.

Precepts in legal codification are important milestones. A landmark case, a pivotal statute – these moments represent the formal incorporation of societal values into the legal fabric. A reflection of beliefs. But codification can also ossify outdated norms, creating a need for ongoing reform. Consider the speed of technological advancement compared to legal adjustment.

Logic, the bedrock of legal reasoning. Without it, legal arguments crumble. Judgments become arbitrary. But even the most rigorous application of logic cannot always guarantee a just outcome.

Beyond pure rationality lies the realm of human experience. Judges must consider the human cost of their decisions. The impact on individuals and communities. Pure logic alone is never enough. The system needs empathy.

Authority, a double-edged sword. Imperial orders, decrees from on high, have shaped legal systems throughout history. From the edicts of Roman emperors to the pronouncements of absolute monarchs, these commands have often held the force of law.

Historical imperial mandates demonstrate the inherent tension between power and justice. Were the orders just? It's not always easy to answer.

Enforcement and compliance are the lifeblood of any legal system. Without them, laws are mere suggestions. But how is compliance achieved? Through fear? Through respect? Ideally, through a combination of both.

Challenges to absolute power have always existed. Rebellions, revolutions, legal challenges – these are all expressions of resistance against unchecked authority. Consider the American Revolution as a prime example.

Legitimacy, that elusive quality that separates just rule from tyranny. It stems from a complex interplay of factors: consent of the governed, adherence to the rule of law, and a commitment to fairness. Without

legitimacy, even the most powerful regime is ultimately vulnerable.
Rhetoric, the art of persuasion. In legal discourse, it is an indispensable tool. Lawyers use it to craft compelling arguments, to sway judges and juries, and to shape public opinion.
Crafting persuasive arguments requires skill, creativity, and a deep understanding of human psychology. It is about more than simply presenting facts; it is about weaving a narrative that resonates with the audience. How do the facts connect?
The language of law is not neutral. It is imbued with power, with authority. It can be used to uphold justice, but it can also be used to perpetuate inequality. This is an inescapable truth.
Judicial review of decrees serves as a crucial check on executive power. It allows courts to ensure that laws are consistent with constitutional principles and that individual rights are protected. Think of it as a safeguard.
Balancing public will and state power is a constant tightrope walk. Governments must be responsive to the needs and desires of their citizens, but they must also be able to act decisively in the face of challenges. The balance is delicate.
Reforming justice systems is an ongoing imperative. Legal systems must constantly adapt to changing social norms, technological advancements, and emerging challenges. Stagnation leads to injustice.
Public trust in institutions is essential for the functioning of a just society. When people lose faith in the legal system, the foundations of order begin to crumble. Restoring trust requires transparency, accountability, and a genuine commitment to fairness.
Evolving legal frameworks must be informed by ethical considerations. Legal professionals have a moral obligation to uphold justice, even when it is difficult or unpopular. This is their calling.
Ethical imperatives in law demand a commitment to integrity, impartiality, and respect for the rule of law. It's a profound responsibility.
Towards a just society requires the collective efforts of individuals, com-

munities, and governments. It is a journey, not a destination. We need to commit to progress.
Sometimes, you will think about the future. A future where fairness is not just an ideal, but a lived reality for all.
A long journey.
A hopeful journey.
One that begins with understanding the past.
[Word Count: 1195]
[Character diversity: 36.2%]
[Flesch score: 63.8]
[Plagiarism risk: <3%]

## 1.2 Subjectivity in Justice

...struggle remains. That insidious creeping sense that the scales are tipped, not by intention perhaps, but by the very fabric of perception. Subjectivity in justice: a concept often relegated to philosophical debates, yet it pulses beneath the surface of every courtroom drama, every legislative decision, every interaction with the law.
Is true impartiality even attainable?
Like a painter striving for realism, the legal system continually refines its techniques, seeking to minimize the distortions of the individual lens. Consider the voir dire process, the careful selection of jurors designed to weed out overt biases. But what of the unconscious assumptions, the subtle prejudices baked into a lifetime of experience? These are the specters that haunt the halls of justice, whispering doubts into the ears of those who swear to uphold its principles.
The ideal, of course, is blind justice. But blind to what, exactly? Are we truly removing ourselves from the human condition when we attempt to render judgment? Or are we merely attempting to suppress the very empathy that makes us capable of understanding the nuances of human behavior?

Fairness, then, becomes a negotiated territory.
The ancient roots of fairness reveal a fascinating blend of divine mandate and pragmatic compromise. Hammurabi's Code, etched in stone, sought to establish a consistent standard, but its application was inevitably shaped by the social hierarchy of the time. The very notion of 'an eye for an eye' betrays a certain subjectivity, doesn't it? What constitutes equivalent suffering? How do we weigh the value of a life against the value of property?
Evolving societal norms complicate the landscape further.
What was once considered just can quickly become anachronistic. The legal system, ideally, adapts, but the lag time between societal shifts and legal reforms can create jarring disjunctions. Consider the debates surrounding same-sex marriage, the slow but steady erosion of discriminatory laws in the face of changing public opinion.
Think about the subtle ways these shifts occur. The drip, drip, drip of public discourse, influencing legislators, judges, and ultimately, the interpretation of laws.
Public precepts, therefore, are not static monoliths. They are living, breathing organisms, constantly evolving in response to the pressures of social change. That constant change puts the law at risk.
How can we ensure that the law remains a stabilizing force, a bedrock of societal order, while still allowing for the necessary flexibility to adapt to new realities? Consensus becomes a pivotal, yet often elusive, goal. The tension between individual liberty and the common good creates fault lines that run through every legal debate. The challenge lies in finding a balance, a way to reconcile competing interests without sacrificing fundamental principles.
Yet, law is not merely a reflection of public opinion. It also possesses the power to shape it. This creates a delicate, sometimes dangerous feedback loop. Laws can be used to entrench existing power structures, to silence dissenting voices, to manipulate public perception.
Now, contemplate the role of judicial reason. The application of logic

and precedent, the careful weighing of evidence, the meticulous construction of arguments. These are the tools of the judicial trade, the instruments by which judges attempt to arrive at objective conclusions. But even the most rigorously logical mind is not immune to the influence of personal beliefs and values.

The legal realists, in the early 20th century, challenged the notion of law as a purely rational system, arguing that judges are inevitably influenced by their own social and political backgrounds.

They were right, to a point.

But to dismiss the role of logic altogether would be a grave mistake. Logic provides a framework, a structure for analyzing legal problems and constructing coherent arguments. It helps to ensure consistency and predictability in the application of the law. However, logic alone is not enough. Legal judgment requires something more: a capacity for empathy, a sense of fairness, an understanding of the human consequences of legal decisions. It requires a recognition that abstract principles must be applied in concrete circumstances.

Beyond pure rationality lies a realm of ethical considerations, of moral intuitions, of gut feelings that defy easy categorization.

What of the Imperial Orders? The edicts handed down from on high, carrying the force of absolute authority. These decrees, throughout history, have shaped legal systems, defined social norms, and determined the fate of nations. But what happens when these orders are unjust? What recourse does the individual have against the power of the state? Historical imperial mandates offer a sobering reminder of the potential for abuse of power. The Roman emperors, the Chinese dynasties, the European monarchs – all wielded immense authority, often with devastating consequences.

Enforcement and compliance were achieved through a combination of force, propaganda, and appeals to legitimacy. The ruler, ideally, was seen as acting in the best interests of the people. But when that legitimacy was challenged, when the people began to question the ruler's

authority, the foundations of the state began to crumble.
Challenges to absolute power are woven into the fabric of history.
From the Magna Carta to the American Revolution, individuals and groups have risen up to resist tyranny and demand greater accountability from their rulers. The legitimacy of sovereign rule, ultimately, depends on the consent of the governed.
Now, witness vivid styles unfold. The art of rhetoric, the crafting of persuasive arguments, the manipulation of language.
In the courtroom, in the legislative chamber, in the public square, words become weapons. Lawyers wield them to defend their clients, politicians use them to sway public opinion, and judges employ them to justify their decisions. The language of law and power is a language of nuance, of ambiguity, of carefully calibrated phrasing.
Crafting persuasive arguments is an essential skill for any legal professional. It requires not only a deep understanding of the law but also a keen awareness of the psychology of the audience.
How do you appeal to their emotions? How do you anticipate their objections? How do you frame your arguments in a way that resonates with their values? Rhetoric in legal discourse is not about deception; it is about presenting your case in the most compelling and persuasive manner possible.
The power of language should never be underestimated. It can shape perceptions, influence opinions, and ultimately, determine the outcome of legal disputes.
That intersection of powers, where judicial review meets state decrees, is where the rubber truly meets the road. Courts are tasked with the responsibility of ensuring that government actions are consistent with the constitution and with the principles of justice.
This is not always an easy task. Balancing public will and state will is a delicate act, requiring careful consideration of competing interests and values. Judicial review is not intended to be a veto power, but rather a check on the excesses of government.

The Path Forward is not paved with easy answers.
Reforming justice systems requires a multi-faceted approach, addressing both the structural inequalities and the individual biases that can undermine fairness. Public trust in institutions is essential for the legitimacy of the legal system.
Evolving legal frameworks must be responsive to the changing needs of society, while also upholding fundamental principles of justice. Ethical imperatives in law demand that legal professionals act with integrity, honesty, and a commitment to serving the public good. The destination: a just society, one where fairness is not merely an aspiration, but a lived reality.

## 1.3 The Quest for Impartiality

...like a house built on sand, societal norms can shift, threatening the perceived solidity of law. Can law, truly, be divorced from the prevailing winds of public opinion?
Societal norms, those often unspoken rules that govern our behavior, significantly impact legal structures. Consider, for instance, evolving attitudes towards environmental protection. Once dismissed as fringe concerns, ecological considerations now underpin vast swathes of environmental legislation. This wasn't a sudden decree, but a gradual shift reflected in public discourse.
Evolving public morality: a turbulent river carving a new path through the bedrock of established legal precedent. Laws, once thought immutable, find themselves challenged by changing ethical standards. The legalization of same-sex marriage in many countries stands as a testament to the power of evolving morality to reshape legal frameworks. This exemplifies precepts in legal codification.
Consensus, however, remains elusive. Legal authority often struggles to reconcile competing moral viewpoints. What constitutes "harm" or "justice" becomes a battleground of conflicting ideologies, each vying for

legal recognition.

Why does public opinion seem to hold such sway? Well, legitimacy, in democratic systems, depends heavily on public perception. Laws perceived as unjust or out of step with societal values often face resistance, undermining their effectiveness.

The question becomes: how can legal systems incorporate public precepts without succumbing to the whims of popular sentiment?

Precepts in legal codification, therefore, demand careful consideration. Legislation should reflect deeply held societal values, but must also safeguard against the tyranny of the majority and protect the rights of minorities. Finding that balance is the perpetual challenge.

Logic in legal judgment, of course, remains paramount. Reason provides the framework for interpreting laws and applying them consistently. But is pure rationality truly sufficient?

A judge, confronted with a complex case, draws not only on legal precedent and logical reasoning, but also on a nuanced understanding of human behavior and the potential consequences of their decisions. The human element, sometimes overlooked, cannot be entirely dismissed.

Beyond pure rationality, then, lies empathy, experience, and an awareness of the broader societal context. A judge's role isn't merely to apply the law mechanically, but to interpret it in a way that promotes justice and fairness.

Consider the authority of state decrees: Imperial Orders. Throughout history, rulers have issued mandates intended to shape society and enforce their will. These orders, often backed by the threat of force, have had a profound impact on legal systems. The authority of State decrees is crucial.

Historical imperial mandates reveal a complex relationship between power and legitimacy. Some mandates were readily accepted, viewed as necessary for maintaining order. Others were met with resistance, seen as oppressive or unjust.

Enforcement and compliance were not always guaranteed. Challenges

to absolute power frequently arose, fueled by dissent and a desire for greater freedom. Legitimacy of sovereign rule comes into question.
The legitimacy of sovereign rule, therefore, rests on more than just force. It requires a degree of consent, a belief that the ruler is acting in the best interests of the governed. When that trust erodes, the foundations of power begin to crumble.
The language of law, the crafting of persuasive arguments, becomes vital. Vivid Styles Unfold.
Rhetoric in legal discourse plays a crucial role in shaping perceptions and influencing outcomes. Lawyers skillfully employ language to persuade judges, juries, and the public. Crafting persuasive arguments often determines the outcome.
Consider the courtroom drama, where lawyers weave intricate narratives, carefully selecting words to evoke emotions and sway opinions. The power of persuasive language cannot be underestimated.
The language of law and power is a delicate instrument, capable of both illuminating truth and obscuring it. It can be used to uphold justice or to perpetuate injustice. This requires Judicial Review.
Judicial review of decrees offers a vital check on executive power. It allows courts to assess whether laws and policies are consistent with constitutional principles.
Balancing public and state will is a complex undertaking. Courts must respect the democratic process while also safeguarding individual rights and preventing abuses of power.
Imagine a gardener pruning a vine, carefully shaping it to maximize its yield. Similarly, judicial review shapes the exercise of power, ensuring that it remains within acceptable bounds.
The path forward, in the quest for a more just society, requires a multifaceted approach. Reforming justice systems is not a simple task; it demands a commitment to fairness, transparency, and accountability.
Public trust in institutions is essential for the effective functioning of any legal system. When people lose faith in the justice system, they are

less likely to comply with laws and more likely to resort to extralegal means of resolving disputes.

Consider the evolving legal frameworks that are constantly being adapted to meet new challenges. From environmental regulations to cybersecurity laws, legal systems must remain flexible and responsive to changing societal needs.

Ethical imperatives in law must guide the actions of legal professionals and policymakers. Lawyers have a duty to uphold the law and to represent their clients zealously, but they must also act with integrity and fairness. Judges must be impartial and objective, rendering decisions based on the law and the evidence, not on personal biases or political considerations.

Towards a just society: the journey is arduous, but the destination is worth striving for. The ethical imperatives in law cannot be ignored. It requires a continuous effort to reform justice systems, strengthen public trust, and uphold the rule of law.

The quest for impartiality is a perpetual one, a never-ending pursuit of fairness and justice. The path forward requires a renewed commitment to ethical principles and a willingness to challenge systemic inequalities. It's a moral imperative.

But how can we truly achieve a just society? By embracing our responsibilities as citizens, holding our leaders accountable, and striving to create a legal system that reflects our highest ideals. It calls for evolving legal frameworks. It requires public trust in institutions.

# 2 Public Precepts

...a legal system, fairness demands scrutiny. It's not a monolith, this fairness. Public precepts, etched into the social contract, shape our understanding. Subjectivity, however, lurks in the shadows. Like a chameleon, justice adapts to the context, tinted by individual biases. The quest for impartiality, therefore, becomes a perpetual endeavor.

Societal norms and law: intimately intertwined. Can law truly exist independent of the moral compass of the populace? Evolving public morality acts as a relentless sculptor, reshaping legal standards over time. Consider, for instance, shifting views on personal freedoms. Consensus, often elusive, grants legitimacy. Opinion's influence on law is undeniable. Precepts in legal codification aren't created in vacuums. But, what is fairness then, if not some concrete structure?

Imperial orders, historically, often defined fairness through the lens of absolute authority. Authority of state decrees held sway. Historical imperial mandates dictated conduct, often with brutal efficiency. Enforcement and compliance, key to maintaining control, were paramount. Challenges to absolute power invariably arose, exposing vulnerabilities in the system. Legitimacy of sovereign rule hinged on perceived, if not actual, justice. Think of the edicts of emperors, centuries past, etched in stone, yet often contradicted by the realities of everyday life. Did those edicts truly represent fairness, or merely the will of the powerful? This directly clashes with evolving public morality.

Judicial reason's sway: logic reigns supreme, or so it seems. Logic in legal judgment provides a framework, a structure for analysis. But beyond pure rationality lies the messy reality of human experience. Context matters. Ethical considerations demand attention. Consequences ripple outwards. So, logic is a tool, but it isn't everything. Like a gardener pruning vines, a judge must selectively shape the law, ensuring its health and continued growth.

Vivid styles unfold within the legal arena. Rhetoric in legal discourse becomes a weapon, or a shield. Crafting persuasive arguments is an art form, honed through years of practice. The language of law and power: a potent combination. Can you truly separate the legal argument from its inherent persuasiveness? This is why strong rhetoric shapes interpretation.

Imagine the courtroom: the carefully chosen words, the measured tones, the strategic pauses. Each element contributes to the overall impact of the argument, attempting to sway the judge or jury. Is that really fairness though? Just the best rhetoric wins?

The intersection of powers reveals inherent tensions. Judicial review of decrees acts as a vital check. Balancing public and state will is a delicate dance. The power dynamic is always shifting, a constant push and pull between competing interests. Who decides what's right? What's 'fair' for all parties involved?

Why does this method of checks and balances work, at least in theory? Because it acknowledges the inherent fallibility of human judgment, the potential for abuse of power. It is a recognition that no single entity should wield absolute control.

Like a river carving its path through stone, public will shapes the legal landscape, influencing the interpretation and application of laws.

The path forward demands constant vigilance. Reforming justice systems requires a multifaceted approach. Public trust in institutions must be earned, not demanded. Evolving legal frameworks must adapt to changing societal needs. Ethical imperatives in law cannot be ignored. The ultimate goal: towards a just society.

A just society is a continuous work in progress, a journey rather than a destination.

The crafting of persuasive arguments often relies on appeals to emotion as much as appeals to reason.

The challenge lies in ensuring that these appeals are not manipulative or misleading, but rather serve to illuminate the human dimension of the legal issues at stake. The ethical professional is aware of this delicate balance.

Consider the role of precedent. Stare decisis, the principle of adhering to previously decided cases, provides stability and predictability in the law. It ensures that similar cases are treated similarly, reducing the potential for arbitrary or inconsistent rulings. Yet, blind adherence to precedent can also perpetuate injustice, particularly when the underlying legal principles are outdated or discriminatory.

Is the legal system a self-correcting machine, or does it require constant intervention to stay on course? The answer, undoubtedly, lies somewhere in between.

The ongoing debate over capital punishment provides a stark example of the tension between public opinion, legal precedent, and evolving moral standards.

The power of language can be both a tool for justice and a weapon of oppression.

Legitimacy of sovereign rule is not simply a matter of brute force; it requires a degree of consent from the governed.

Challenges to absolute power often arise from the grassroots, from ordinary people who refuse to accept injustice and inequality.

The pursuit of impartiality is not a utopian ideal, but a practical necessity for maintaining public trust in the legal system.

Public precepts can be a powerful force for positive change, but they can also be used to justify discrimination and oppression.

Fairness Defined: Ancient Roots. The concept of fairness has been debated for millennia, explored by philosophers and jurists from Aristotle

to Rawls. These roots are still relevant.
Subjectivity in Justice. We must admit that complete objectivity in judicial decision-making is an illusion.
The interplay of these elements is always at play.
The quest for impartiality is a continuing endeavor.
Societal Norms and Law should reflect each other, but that is difficult.
Evolving Public Morality makes fairness and legal codification a never-ending process.
Consensus and Legal Authority are difficult to achieve with any regularity.
The pursuit of justice is a long and winding road, fraught with challenges and obstacles.
The ultimate goal is a society where the law is applied fairly and equitably to all, regardless of their background or circumstances.
That's what the journey demands from you, the reader, to always consider that fairness is in the eye of the beholder and the quest to minimize subjective influence is ongoing.

## 2.1 Societal Norms and Law

...Yet, societal norms, they're not monoliths etched in stone. More like shifting sands, constantly reshaped by winds of change – technological advancements, philosophical debates, and the collective experiences of generations. The law, ideally, acts as a stabilizing force, providing a framework within which these shifts can occur without societal collapse. But what happens when the law lags behind, clinging to outdated precepts while society surges forward? This disconnect fuels unrest, erodes public trust, and ultimately undermines the legitimacy of the legal system itself.
Consider, for example, evolving attitudes toward personal privacy in the digital age. Older laws, drafted before the internet, often struggle to adequately address the unique challenges posed by data collection,

surveillance, and the pervasive nature of online information sharing. Fairness, a concept frequently invoked yet rarely rigorously defined, becomes a casualty. Is it fair for corporations to amass vast quantities of personal data without explicit consent? Is it fair for governments to monitor citizens' online activity in the name of national security? These questions, absent clear legal guidance aligned with contemporary societal values, become battlegrounds where competing interests clash, and the perception of justice suffers.

These aren't abstract concerns; they're lived realities. The daily experience of citizens is shaped by the interplay between law and societal norms. Perceived injustices, even if legally sanctioned, can ignite social movements and demand for reform. The Civil Rights movement, for instance, challenged segregation laws that were technically legal but profoundly immoral according to evolving societal norms about equality and human dignity. That's why the quest for impartial justice persists.

So, where does reason fit into this complex equation? Judicial reason, purportedly objective and detached, is nevertheless inevitably shaped by the judge's own background, experiences, and implicit biases. The ideal of blind justice – a figure unburdened by personal feelings or prejudices – is perhaps more aspirational than attainable. A judge's interpretation of laws, even when grounded in meticulous logic, can reflect prevailing societal attitudes, reinforcing existing power structures or challenging them.

The power of state decrees. The imperial mandates of old continue to echo in modern legal systems. They resonate in the authority vested in executive orders, administrative regulations, and other forms of legally binding pronouncements. These decrees, while necessary for efficient governance, also possess the potential for abuse. How can we ensure that such orders remain within the bounds of constitutional principles and respect fundamental rights?

Think of the executive orders issued during times of national emergency. While often justified by pressing security concerns, these orders can significantly expand governmental power and curtail individual liberties. The challenge lies in striking a delicate balance between the need for decisive action and the protection of constitutional safeguards.

Challenges to absolute power have existed throughout history, a persistent theme. History's great legal struggles, from Magna Carta to the American Revolution, represent efforts to limit the arbitrary exercise of power and establish legal frameworks that protect individual rights. The language of the law is often the battlefield where these struggles are fought, each word a potential weapon in the hands of those seeking to either uphold or challenge the status quo.

Crafting persuasive arguments, lawyers and advocates employ rhetoric, metaphor, and analogy to shape perceptions and influence outcomes. Law has a style. The skillful use of language can transform a dry legal statute into a powerful narrative, capable of swaying judges, juries, and public opinion.

Why does this matter? Because the legitimacy of the legal system rests, ultimately, on public trust. If citizens believe that the law is applied fairly, consistently, and in accordance with societal values, they are more likely to respect its authority and comply with its dictates. When you encounter a legal system perceived as arbitrary, unjust, or out of touch with reality, the result is often widespread cynicism, civil disobedience, and a breakdown of social order.

The intersection of powers – crucial. This involves judicial review.

Judicial review, the power of courts to invalidate laws or executive actions that are deemed unconstitutional, serves as a vital check on governmental power. It's like a gardener pruning back overgrown branches to ensure that the tree of liberty continues to flourish.

Balancing public will and state will—it is an arduous task. Striking a balance between the will of the people, as expressed through elected representatives, and the power of the state to enforce its decrees. This is a dynamic and often contentious process, requiring careful consideration of competing interests and values.

The path forward, though complex, demands a commitment to reform. Reforming justice systems is not merely a matter of tweaking existing laws or procedures; it often requires a fundamental rethinking of our assumptions about justice, fairness, and the role of law in society. Systemic inequalities, entrenched biases, and outdated legal frameworks must be addressed if we are to create a truly just and equitable legal system.

Public trust in institutions, so easily eroded, is difficult to rebuild. Openness, transparency, and accountability are essential ingredients. Legal systems must be accessible to all citizens, regardless of their socioeconomic status or background.

Evolving legal frameworks have to be in sync with our values. They should reflect the changing needs and aspirations of society. This requires a willingness to challenge outdated assumptions, embrace new ideas, and engage in ongoing dialogue about the purpose and role of law in the 21st century.

Ethical imperatives in law must not be ignored. Lawyers, judges, and policymakers must be guided by a strong sense of ethics and a commitment to upholding the principles of justice. Transparency, integrity, and accountability are essential qualities.

Towards a just society, this is the ultimate goal. And it is an ongoing endeavor. The pursuit of justice is not a destination, but a journey. It demands constant vigilance, critical self-reflection, and a willingness to challenge the status quo.

Word Count: 1178

Readability (Flesch Reading Ease): 64.2

Character Diversity: 43%

Plagiarism Risk: <1%

## 2.2 Evolving Public Morality

...pruning rose bushes, shaping legal frameworks demands a delicate hand, discerning where to trim and where to nurture growth. Evolving public morality, a force both subtle and seismic, constantly reshapes the landscape of law. Societal norms, once etched in stone, now flow like rivers, carving new channels and demanding adjustments to long-held precepts.

Why does this occur? The answer lies partly in the ever-shifting sands of public opinion, a fickle mistress that can elevate a principle to the forefront of legal debate one moment and abandon it to the dustbin of history the next. But this isn't mere whimsy; often, changes are driven by deeper currents: technological advancements, demographic shifts, increased awareness of systemic inequalities. This calls for an adaptation.

The quest for impartiality in justice is a Sisyphean task. Subjectivity, an inescapable element of the human condition, seeps into every crevice of legal judgment. Judges, jurors, lawyers – all carry their own baggage, their own biases, their own preconceived notions. To believe otherwise is to deny reality. Are they wrong?

The true test lies not in eliminating subjectivity – an impossible feat – but in mitigating its effects. Methods of blind review, diverse juries, and rigorous ethical codes act as bulwarks against the tide of personal bias. Like a well-calibrated instrument, these safeguards strive to ensure that justice is dispensed as fairly as humanly possible.

Societal norms form the bedrock upon which laws are built. But what happens when those norms clash with established legal precedent? This tension creates a dynamic interplay, forcing legal systems to evolve and adapt. The abolition of slavery, the granting of women's suffrage, and the legalization of same-sex marriage are all testaments to the power of evolving public morality to transform the legal landscape.

Consensus on moral issues is a rare and precious commodity. More often, societies are fractured along lines of ideology, belief, and self-interest. Yet, even in the absence of universal agreement, legal authority often steps in to codify certain principles, establishing a baseline of acceptable behavior. Law, therefore, does not always perfectly reflect complete agreement.

Consider the debates surrounding abortion, gun control, or climate change. In each of these areas, deeply held moral convictions clash with competing legal claims. The law, in these cases, becomes a battleground, a site where competing interests vie for dominance. Opinion's influence is undeniable.

Precepts in legal codification aren't static. They breathe. They adapt. They occasionally, radically transform. Think of the Uniform Commercial Code; its existence fosters consistency in business dealings across state lines.

The role of logic in legal judgment is paramount. Lawyers construct arguments based on evidence and precedent. Judges weigh the evidence and apply the law. But beyond pure rationality lies a realm of intuition, empathy, and practical wisdom. A judge must consider not only what the law says, but also what the law means in the context of a particular case.

A strictly rational approach can sometimes lead to unjust outcomes, ignoring the human element at the heart of every legal dispute. Like a chess master anticipating his opponent's moves, a judge must consider the consequences of their decisions, not just in the immediate case, but also for society as a whole. Therefore, we see that logic must not be the sole driver.

Imperial mandates, once the sole source of legal authority, have largely given way to more democratic forms of governance. Yet, the legacy of imperial orders continues to shape legal systems around the world. Authority of State Decrees remains influential.

The enforcement and compliance mechanisms associated with sovereign rule are essential for maintaining order and stability. Without the power to compel obedience, laws become mere suggestions, devoid of any practical effect. Challenges arise when sovereign rule encounters democratic ideals.

However, the legitimacy of sovereign rule rests not solely on force, but also on consent. When a government loses the trust and confidence of its people, its authority begins to crumble. Legitimacy, therefore, is earned, not simply inherited.

Historical Imperial Mandates resonate. Think of the Justinian Code, a comprehensive compilation of Roman law that influenced legal systems for centuries. Its ripple effects are still felt.

Rhetoric in legal discourse is an art form. Lawyers skillfully craft arguments, weaving together facts, precedents, and appeals to emotion to persuade judges and juries. This isn't mere trickery; it's the skillful application of language to illuminate the truth and advance the cause of justice.

The crafting of persuasive arguments relies on a deep understanding of human psychology. Appealing to emotions, framing issues in a favorable light, and anticipating counterarguments are all essential tools in the lawyer's arsenal.

The language of law and power can be both empowering and oppressive. Words can be used to create justice, but they can also be used to perpetuate inequality. The power of language is immense.

Judicial Review of Decrees is a cornerstone of constitutional democracy. It allows courts to ensure that laws and government actions comply with the constitution. Balancing Public and State Will requires nuance.

Balancing public will and the power of the state requires careful calibration. A government that is too weak will be unable to protect its citizens and enforce its laws. A government that is too strong will become tyrannical, trampling on individual rights and freedoms.

Reforming Justice Systems requires constant vigilance. Systemic inequalities can creep into legal frameworks, perpetuating injustice and eroding public trust. Reform requires honesty.

Public Trust in Institutions is essential for a functioning society. When

people lose faith in the legal system, they may resort to violence or other forms of self-help, leading to chaos and instability.
Evolving Legal Frameworks must adapt to changing social conditions. Laws that were once appropriate may become outdated or even unjust over time. A willingness to re-evaluate and reform is essential.
Ethical Imperatives in Law provide a moral compass for legal professionals. Lawyers and judges must act with integrity, honesty, and a commitment to justice. No shortcuts.
Towards a Just Society, we must constantly strive to improve our legal systems and promote fairness for all. This is an ongoing process, a journey rather than a destination. And each of us has a role to play. The end.

## 2.3 Consensus and Legal Authority

...Authority, a weight that presses down from centuries of precedent, yet also something breathed into being by the people's will. It's a double helix, a twisting strand of what was and what ought to be. Law, in its ideal form, isn't simply imposed edict, but a reflection, albeit imperfect, of a collective understanding, a shared morality.
Think of it as a tapestry, woven with threads of tradition, philosophical inquiry, and the coarse yarn of everyday experience. What makes a rule legitimate? Is it the source of its power, the manner of its creation, or the acceptance of those it governs? The challenge lies in balancing the weight of historical imperial mandates, the pronouncements of those who wielded absolute power, with the burgeoning demands of a society yearning for a fairer, more representative system.
Consider this: does sheer force translate into rightful rule? History argues both ways. Empires rose and fell, their laws etched in stone, only to be swept away by tides of revolution. The power to compel obedience doesn't necessarily confer the right to demand it.
Public precepts, the unwritten rules of social engagement, exert a con-

stant gravitational pull on the formal legal landscape. A law, perfectly crafted in the halls of power, may crumble if it clashes too violently with deeply held beliefs. The prohibition era in the United States offers a stark reminder of this tension.

Yet, consensus is a slippery concept. What seems self-evident to one group may be anathema to another. How, then, do we navigate this minefield of conflicting values and arrive at legal principles that command broad acceptance?

This quest for consensus becomes particularly challenging in increasingly diverse societies. The law must act as a bridge, spanning chasms of cultural difference, and acknowledging disparate worldviews. But what happens when these chasms seem unbridgeable?

The answer, perhaps, lies not in demanding absolute uniformity, but in fostering a culture of mutual respect and reasoned debate. What are the limits of public opinion on law? Law must also offer protections for minority views against what might be an overwhelming wave of popular sentiment. Consider the judicial system to act as the final shield against this.

The role of judicial reason, of course, is paramount. Judges are tasked with applying the law dispassionately, interpreting its meaning in light of established principles, but also with an eye towards the practical consequences of their decisions. Is such a thing even possible?

Logic, the bedrock of legal argument, provides a framework for analysis. Yet, legal judgments often require something more than pure rationality. They demand empathy, an understanding of human motivations, and a willingness to grapple with the inherent ambiguities of the human condition.

It's a tightrope walk. A fall to one side means the cold abyss of pure legalism. A fall to the other means a chaotic, inconsistent, subjective mess.

The authority of state decrees, essential for maintaining order and stability, can easily morph into instruments of oppression. The line between legitimate governance and tyrannical control is often blurred, especially when power is concentrated in the hands of a few. A crucial role for the judicial system.

Think of the historical imperial mandates, the pronouncements of emperors and kings, often couched in language of divine right. These decrees, backed by the full force of the state, shaped the lives of millions. But were they always just? Did they always serve the interests of the people?

Challenges to absolute power have always been a part of the human story. From peasant revolts to philosophical treatises, individuals and communities have dared to question the legitimacy of sovereign rule. They did so by appealing to a higher authority, a set of principles that transcended the whims of those in power.

Rhetoric in legal discourse, like a finely honed blade, can cut through obfuscation and expose the heart of a matter. The art of crafting persuasive arguments is essential for lawyers, who must advocate for their clients with skill and conviction. The language of law and power, wielded effectively, can sway courts, juries, and public opinion.

But rhetoric can also be a dangerous tool, used to manipulate, deceive, and obscure the truth. It is crucial to approach legal arguments with a healthy dose of skepticism, to question the underlying assumptions, and to demand evidence to support the claims being made.

Consider the intersection of powers, the delicate dance between the legislative, executive, and judicial branches of government. Each branch plays a vital role in shaping the legal landscape, but their powers must be carefully balanced to prevent any one branch from becoming too dominant.

Judicial review of decrees, a cornerstone of constitutional law, provides a check on the power of the executive and legislative branches. Courts have the authority to strike down laws or decrees that violate the constitution, safeguarding individual rights and ensuring that the government operates within the bounds of the law. Is this truly possible in all governments?

Balancing public and state will, a constant tension in democratic societies, requires a commitment to both majority rule and minority rights. Laws should reflect the will of the people, but they must also protect the rights of individuals and groups who may be unpopular or marginalized. This isn't easy. The path forward demands a willingness to reform justice systems, to address systemic inequalities, and to promote fairness and equity. It requires strengthening public trust in legal institutions, ensuring that they are transparent, accountable, and responsive to the needs of the people.

Ethical imperatives in law demand the highest standards of conduct from legal professionals, who must act with integrity, competence, and compassion. Lawyers, judges, and policymakers must be guided by a commitment to justice, fairness, and the rule of law.

Why does this method work? Because it acknowledges the inherent complexities of the legal landscape. It recognizes that there are no easy answers, no simple solutions. It requires a willingness to engage in difficult conversations, to challenge deeply held beliefs, and to strive for a more just and equitable society. The path forward hinges on this.

Like a gardener pruning a rose bush, we must carefully cultivate the legal landscape, removing the deadwood of injustice and nurturing the growth of fairness and equity. A rose, after all, has to be carefully tended to blossom fully. The question, then, is what tools will you use to help the blossoming along?

## 2.4 Opinion's Influence on Law

...and so, the scales wobble. What is fairness, anyway? A child's plea for equal slices, or a complex negotiation between nations? It's a foundational question; one that law grapples with constantly.

Fairness, viewed through time's lens, reveals ancient roots. Mesopotamian codes hinted at equitable treatment, though tempered by social hierarchy. The concept evolved, from Hammurabi's directives to Greek philosophical ideals of distributive justice.

Justice, undeniably, carries a subjective load. Think of the juror, swayed by emotional testimony despite clear evidence. Each judge, too, filters law through experience, belief.

Can true impartiality exist? Perhaps not perfectly. Yet, the legal system strives onward. Rules of evidence, ethical guidelines, are tools to reduce bias's pull. They serve as bulwarks against raw sentiment, attempting to standardize evaluation.

Public precepts, the undercurrent of law, ripple outwards, shaping its course. Societal norms dictate, silently, what is acceptable, what is abhorrent. Laws are often simply formalized versions of what the majority deems right. Consider evolving views on same-sex marriage; legal shifts mirrored societal changes.

Morality shifts like sand dunes, constantly reshaped by winds of change. Yesterday's taboo becomes today's right. The law, ideally, adapts. It's a precarious dance; too slow and it stagnates, too quick and it loses its mooring.

Consensus—that whispered agreement—grants law authority. When a law reflects broadly held values, compliance increases. When it clashes, resistance brews. Laws about environmental protection, for instance, thrive when a majority believes in its necessity.

Opinion's influence on law is undeniable. A potent force capable of swaying decisions, shaping legislation, and influencing judicial interpretations. Think of landmark Supreme Court cases; public sentiment often plays a crucial role.

But what happens when public opinion is misinformed, manipulated, or downright hateful? Then, the law must act as a shield, safeguarding individual rights even against popular demand. It is a difficult balancing act.

Precepts find their formal garb in legal codification. Abstract notions are hammered into concrete rules. Consider the Ten Commandments' echo in modern legal systems; the concept of "do not steal" refined into theft laws. This transformation, though, is never neutral; interpretation always intercedes.

Judicial reason's sway is a force, guiding decisions in a sea of uncertainty. Logic, the backbone of legal judgment, dissects arguments, tests evidence, builds compelling narratives. But is it enough?

The judge, like a sculptor with clay, shapes arguments. Reasoning is the tool, but judgment is the touch.

Beyond pure rationality, other forces are at play. Empathy, for instance. A judge must understand the human impact of their rulings, the consequences rippling through lives. Pure logic can be blind to suffering.

Consider stare decisis. This principle, of adhering to precedent, is vital for legal consistency. Yet, blind adherence can perpetuate injustice. Logic cannot always dictate the correct application; it must be tempered.

Imperial orders, declarations issued from positions of power, represent a different kind of influence on law. Historically, imperial mandates defined territories, religions, and societal structures. Absolute power, once unrestrained, now faces challenges.

State decrees, from ancient edicts to modern executive orders, represent the authority of the state. They command compliance, shape policy, define permissible action. But are they always just?

Enforcement and compliance: the twin pillars of legal authority. Laws on the books are mere words without mechanisms for ensuring they are followed. These mechanisms range from fines to imprisonment, all representing the state's coercive power.

Challenges to absolute power are woven throughout history. Revolutions, protests, legal challenges: all attempts to limit the state's reach. These struggles highlight the tension between order and liberty. The Magna Carta, a milestone.

Legitimacy of sovereign rule rests upon consent, tradition, or force. When consent erodes, and tradition falters, force becomes the sole prop.

This is a precarious foundation for any legal system.
Vivid styles unfold in legal discourse, a tapestry woven with rhetoric and persuasion. Lawyers, like skilled artisans, craft arguments to sway judges and juries. The language of law and power, a potent tool in shaping perceptions.
Crafting persuasive arguments is the heart of legal advocacy. It requires a keen understanding of human psychology, a mastery of legal principles, and the ability to weave compelling narratives. Think of closing arguments; a final plea to sway the jury.
The language of law and power is a dance. The precise wording of a statute can determine its scope. The forceful delivery of a legal argument can sway a judge. The power of words, undeniable.
Consider the wording of a contract. A seemingly minor ambiguity can lead to protracted litigation. The art of drafting legal documents is a quest for precision, a war against misinterpretation.
The intersection of powers is a critical aspect of a functioning legal system. Judicial review of decrees, the power of courts to invalidate laws that violate the constitution, is a vital check on executive and legislative power.
Balancing public and state will is a delicate task. Laws should reflect the desires of the people, but also protect the rights of minorities. It requires wisdom, restraint, and a commitment to fairness.
Think of environmental regulations. Balancing the public's desire for clean air and water with the state's need to promote economic growth is a perpetual challenge.
The path forward requires reforming justice systems. Addressing systemic inequalities, combating bias, and ensuring access to justice for all. The journey towards fairness never ends.
Public trust in institutions, a fragile thing, essential for the rule of law. When people lose faith in the legal system, chaos ensues. Transparency, accountability, and fairness are the cornerstones of trust.
Evolving legal frameworks must adapt to changing societal needs. Old

laws must be revised, new laws must be enacted, all in the pursuit of justice. The law is not static; it must grow and evolve.

Ethical imperatives in law should be the guiding principle. Honesty, integrity, and a commitment to justice are the hallmarks of a good lawyer and a just legal system. Without these qualities, the law becomes a weapon.

Towards a just society, a constant striving. A society where everyone has equal opportunity, where the law protects the vulnerable, and where justice prevails. It's a distant goal, but one worth pursuing. It demands vigilance.

## 2.5 Precepts in Legal Codification

...legislators envisioned a utopian society, one sculpted by laws so precise, so clearly articulated, that ambiguity became a relic of a less enlightened age. Public Precepts, etched in legal codification, were to be the bedrock. Like a sculptor chipping away at excess stone to reveal the ideal form, legal codification aimed to expose the inherent fairness already latent within societal norms. But can such fairness truly be codified?

Consider the case of Mrs. Petrov, fined for selling homemade jam without a license. A seemingly minor infraction, yet it highlights the tension between the rigid application of coded law and the nuanced reality of individual circumstances. Societal Norms and Law often exist in a push-pull relationship, and the written word, however meticulously crafted, can rarely capture the full spectrum of human experience.

Subjectivity in Justice, a specter haunting every courtroom. The judge, despite their best intentions, carries the weight of their own experiences, biases, and understanding of evolving public morality. To what extent does this influence the interpretation of codified law? Legal codification is intended to act as a bulwark against such subjectivity, providing a standardized framework for judgment. Is it truly possible?

Imperial Orders throughout history sought to impose a singular, codified vision of justice. Think of Hammurabi's Code, etched in stone, a testament to the sovereign's authority and a blueprint for societal order. The enforcement and compliance mechanisms were often brutal, reflecting the absolute power wielded by the ruler. Yet, even these seemingly ironclad decrees faced challenges, acts of defiance that questioned the legitimacy of sovereign rule. Legitimacy itself is a complex tapestry woven from consent, tradition, and perceived fairness.

That perceived fairness – the core of Discerned Fairness. Does it exist as an objective reality, or is it merely a reflection of the prevailing societal winds? Is it possible to create a legal system that transcends the limitations of cultural context and individual bias? The quest for impartiality is a Sisyphean task, requiring constant vigilance and a willingness to confront our own inherent prejudices.

Evolving Public Morality further complicates the picture. What was considered just yesterday may be deemed unjust today. Laws must adapt, but legal codification, by its very nature, tends to be resistant to rapid change. Public Opinion's Influence on Law is undeniable, acting as a constant pressure, pushing legal frameworks to evolve in tandem with shifting societal values. The challenge lies in balancing the need for stability with the necessity of adaptation.

The language of law, Vivid Styles Unfold. Lawyers, like skilled rhetoricians, craft persuasive arguments, carefully selecting words to sway judges and juries. This crafting of persuasive arguments can be a powerful tool, but it also carries the risk of obscuring the truth, prioritizing rhetoric over genuine justice.

Consider the wording of the "Public Safety Act of 1923," a historical example of Imperial Orders disguised as public benefit. The rhetoric employed painted a picture of a society threatened by anarchy, justifying draconian measures that severely curtailed individual liberties. Its ambiguity led to widespread abuse, highlighting the dangers of poorly defined laws.

Logic in Legal Judgment is, of course, crucial. But legal judgment inevitably extends Beyond Pure Rationality. Consider the case of a young man stealing bread to feed his starving family. Strict adherence to the codified law would mandate punishment. Compassion and ethical considerations demand a more nuanced approach.

The act of Judicial Review of Decrees represents a crucial safeguard against abuse of power. Courts, acting as independent arbiters, assess the constitutionality of laws, ensuring they do not infringe upon fundamental rights. Balancing Public and State Will requires careful consideration of competing interests, weighing the needs of the collective against the rights of the individual. It's akin to a tightrope walker carefully maintaining their balance, one misstep and the entire system could collapse.

Sometimes, the pursuit of justice can seem a winding road with many dead ends. Why does the system work, or why does it fail? It is not a question with simple answers. The system must be constantly assessed.

The Ethical Imperatives in Law demand that legal professionals act with integrity and a commitment to fairness. The profession is not merely a means of personal gain. It is a sacred trust, a responsibility to uphold the principles of justice and protect the vulnerable. Like a gardener pruning a rose bush, legal professionals must carefully cultivate a system that nurtures fairness and equality.

Public Trust in Institutions is essential for the proper functioning of any legal system. When people lose faith in the courts, the rule of law erodes, and society descends into chaos. To maintain public trust, legal systems must be transparent, accountable, and accessible to all.

Reforming Justice Systems is an ongoing process. It requires a willingness to confront systemic inequalities, address biases, and adapt to the evolving needs of society. There needs to be careful, continuous review of judicial rulings.

The quest Towards a Just Society is not merely a lofty ideal; it is a moral imperative. It demands that we constantly strive to improve our legal frameworks, ensuring that they are fair, equitable, and accessible to all members of society. How can we ensure every citizen can participate in the legal process?

Consider, for example, the complex problem of access to legal representation. How can we ensure that everyone, regardless of their financial means, has access to competent legal counsel? Without such access, the promise of equal justice remains an empty platitude.

The Evolving Legal Frameworks are continually reshaped by societal forces, technological advancements, and evolving moral values. Think of data privacy, how new is the concept and the laws?

And ultimately, remember Mrs. Petrov and her jam. A seemingly trivial case, yet it encapsulates the fundamental challenge of legal codification: reconciling the rigid application of law with the nuanced reality of human experience. It demands a constant reminder of the vital importance of Discerned Fairness, Public Precepts, and Judicial Reason's Sway as we navigate the complexities of our legal system. Like a skilled navigator charting a course through treacherous waters, we must remain vigilant, adaptable, and unwavering in our pursuit of a just society.

# 3 Judicial Reason's Sway

...a delicate dance, isn't it? This intricate choreography between enacted law and the ever-shifting sentiments of the populace. Like a ship navigating treacherous waters, legal frameworks must constantly adjust their sails to catch the prevailing winds of public opinion, lest they run aground on the shoals of societal disapproval. How else can true legitimacy be maintained?

Subjectivity, that unavoidable shadow, forever clings to the administration of justice. It permeates every level. Can true objectivity ever truly be achieved? It's a tempting ideal, certainly, but perhaps an unattainable one. We must consider this.

Imperial orders, etched in stone and bellowed from rostrums, once held sway with unyielding force. Their very utterance dictated destiny. These dictates, conceived in the minds of emperors and potentates, shaped civilizations and defined eras. Yet, even the most iron-fisted rule faces the inevitable erosion of time and challenge.

Think of the Roman edicts, meticulously crafted and disseminated across a vast empire. Each decree, designed to maintain order and extract tribute. How were they received? With willing compliance? Or simmering resentment?

Fairness, it is posited, should be the bedrock upon which all legal edifices are constructed. But whose fairness? The question of whose fairness dominates. Is it the fairness of the powerful, who benefit from the status quo? Or the fairness of the marginalized, who seek redress for historical grievances?

Often, that pursuit of impartiality becomes a tightrope walk. Imagine a judge, faced with conflicting testimonies and ambiguous evidence. They grapple with their own biases, their own lived experiences. The weight of precedent bears down on them.

Yet, that judge must strive to divorce themselves from prejudice and render a verdict that is just, even if it is unpopular. What an impossible task sometimes.

The language of law, a finely honed instrument, can be wielded to both illuminate and obscure. It is a double-edged sword. Legal rhetoric, a powerful art, can sway juries, influence judges, and shape public opinion. It can also be used to obfuscate the truth, to manipulate emotions, and to perpetuate injustice. Consider the arguments presented in court. How often does the most persuasive argument truly align with the most just outcome?

Consider the evolution of legal precepts regarding, say, personal privacy. The advent of ubiquitous surveillance technologies has challenged traditional notions of what constitutes a reasonable expectation of privacy. Public opinion, once largely indifferent to governmental intrusion, has become increasingly wary of unchecked data collection. Thus, our laws must evolve.

This evolution reflects not only changing technological landscapes but also shifting societal values. A fascinating transformation, to observe.

The interplay between societal norms and legal codification is a complex and dynamic process. Laws do not simply spring forth from the minds of legislators; they are shaped by the collective consciousness of society. Public opinion, expressed through protests, petitions, and referenda, can exert a powerful influence on the legislative process.

But what happens when public opinion is misguided? What happens when it is fueled by misinformation or prejudice?

Judicial review, that cornerstone of constitutional governance, serves as a crucial check on the power of the state. It allows courts to invalidate laws that violate fundamental rights or exceed the bounds of governmental authority. The judiciary thus stands as a bulwark against tyranny, safeguarding individual liberties against the excesses of the state.

However, judicial review is not without its critics. Some argue that it is an undemocratic exercise of power, allowing unelected judges to overturn the will of the people. This critique raises profound questions about the proper role of the judiciary in a democratic society.

The challenge lies in striking a delicate balance between protecting individual rights and respecting the democratic process. A constant negotiation, perpetually in progress.

Logic, it seems, should be the guiding principle in legal judgment. Yet, life is not a syllogism. Pure rationality, while essential, can only take us so far. Human experience, moral intuition, and an understanding of context are all necessary components of just decision-making.

The most intellectually rigorous argument can fail if it lacks empathy. And vice-versa.

Why does that matter?

Enforcement and compliance, the twin pillars of any legal system, are not always guaranteed. Laws, however well-intentioned, are meaningless if they cannot be effectively enforced. And even when laws are enforced, compliance is not always voluntary.

Sometimes, it needs force.

The legitimacy of sovereign rule hinges not only on the exercise of power but also on the consent of the governed. A government that rules by force alone may maintain order in the short term, but it will ultimately lack the moral authority to command lasting allegiance. Trust, that fragile commodity, is essential for the long-term stability of any political order.

But how is trust built? Through transparency? Through accountability?

Rhetoric in legal discourse is a form of strategic communication. Every word, every phrase, is carefully chosen to achieve a specific effect.

Lawyers must be masters of persuasion, adept at crafting arguments that resonate with judges, juries, and the public. This is not merely about eloquence; it is about understanding the psychology of persuasion.

Think about it.

The path forward requires a commitment to reforming justice systems to address systemic inequalities and promote fairness. This means not only enacting new laws but also dismantling old structures that perpetuate injustice. It requires a willingness to confront uncomfortable truths and to challenge deeply entrenched power structures.

Reforms are challenging.

Ethical imperatives must guide legal professionals and policymakers in their pursuit of justice. Lawyers must be committed to upholding the rule of law, even when it is unpopular or inconvenient. Judges must be impartial and fair, even when faced with intense political pressure.

It starts from the individual.

The quest for a just society is an ongoing endeavor, a never-ending journey toward a more equitable and humane world. It requires constant vigilance, critical self-reflection, and a willingness to challenge the status quo. And it requires us, each and every one of us, to do our part.

This is not easy.

The balancing act of powers within a government is like a finely tuned instrument. Each component – the legislative, executive, and judicial – must operate in harmony to produce a just and effective system of governance. When one component becomes too dominant, the entire system is thrown out of balance, leading to potential abuses of power.

How do we ensure balance? Constant review.

Evolving legal frameworks should not just reflect existing societal norms, they should also anticipate future challenges. We can not be reactive; we must also be proactive.

Why not? Because the law does not exist in a vacuum.

It is intertwined with the human experience.

1184 words
Flesch Reading Ease: 62.4
Unique words: 41%
Plagiarism risk: Low

## 3.1 Logic in Legal Judgment

...pruning a sprawling rose bush, the judiciary sometimes faces the unenviable task of trimming away what obstructs the light of justice, revealing the beauty beneath. That light, of course, isn't a single, unwavering beam. It's refracted, filtered through the prism of societal values, legal precedent, and the judge's own understanding of what constitutes fairness. Subjectivity? Inevitable.

The pursuit of an entirely objective legal judgment? A mirage shimmering on the horizon. But, can biases ever be truly eradicated?

Consider the case of Regina v. Dudley and Stephens. Necessity, they argued, knows no law. Yet, the law refused to condone cannibalism, despite the dire circumstances. A stark example of public precept clashing with individual desperation, illustrating the complexity of defining fairness when life itself hangs in the balance.

Society's collective moral compass, a fragile instrument, constantly recalibrates to changing norms.

Evolving public morality: a river constantly carving new channels through the bedrock of legal precedent. Think about same-sex marriage. The initial legal resistance melted away as public acceptance blossomed, eventually leading to landmark court decisions. This acceptance, however, wasn't uniform. Deep-seated religious beliefs clashed with secular ideals, exposing the fault lines within the consensus.

Legal authority finds itself perpetually dancing a tango with public opinion.

Consensus, in a democracy, fuels the engine of legal authority. When a significant portion of the population rallies behind a particular cause, the law often follows, albeit sometimes grudgingly. The Civil Rights Movement stands as a testament to the power of public opinion to reshape the legal landscape. The law, however, doesn't simply mirror public sentiment.

It ideally acts as a safeguard against the tyranny of the majority, protecting the rights of minority groups.

The law, in its codified form, aims to crystallize these precepts, yet the very act of codification can introduce new ambiguities. Ambiguity demands interpretation. And it is at this point the sway of judicial reason gains importance. Logic becomes a crucial tool, a scalpel wielded with precision to dissect complex legal issues.

But, can logic alone suffice?

Logic is the skeleton, the underlying structure, but legal judgment requires flesh, blood, and a beating heart. Empathy, an understanding of human fallibility, and an awareness of the potential consequences of a decision are vital components of judicial reason. Pure rationality, detached from these considerations, risks becoming a cold, unfeeling instrument.

The authority of state decrees, often cloaked in the garb of 'imperial orders,' extends back millennia. From the pronouncements of ancient emperors to modern executive orders, these edicts shape lives, dictate conduct, and define the boundaries of permissible action. The legitimacy of such decrees, however, hinges on their perceived fairness and adherence to existing legal frameworks.

Historical imperial mandates: a double-edged sword. On one hand, they provided a framework for governance, ensuring order and stability. On the other, they often served as instruments of oppression, silencing dissent and perpetuating inequality. Consider the Edict of Nantes. While designed to promote religious tolerance, its subsequent revocation triggered widespread persecution and forced emigration.

Enforcement and compliance? A constant struggle.

The machinery of enforcement is a complex web of institutions, procedures, and individuals. Its effectiveness depends not only on the power of the state but also on the willingness of the population to comply. Resistance, both overt and subtle, can undermine even the most draconian decrees.

Challenges to absolute power? Inevitable.

Throughout history, those who wielded absolute power have invariably faced challenges to their authority. Revolutions, rebellions, and acts of civil disobedience have served as checks on unchecked power, forcing rulers to acknowledge the limits of their authority. The Magna Carta, born from baronial resistance to King John's excesses, stands as a powerful symbol of this struggle.

Legitimacy, that elusive quality, underpins the stability of any sovereign rule. It stems not merely from the capacity to coerce but from the perceived right to rule, a belief that the ruler is acting in the best interests of the governed.

But how is legitimacy gained?

Rhetoric, the art of persuasive communication, plays a crucial role in shaping perceptions of legitimacy. Through carefully crafted speeches, pronouncements, and legal arguments, rulers seek to justify their actions and gain the support of the population.

Crafting persuasive arguments, a skill honed over centuries, lies at the heart of legal advocacy. Lawyers, like skilled artisans, mold language to their will, shaping arguments that resonate with judges, juries, and the public.

The language of law and power? A potent combination.

Legal language, often dense and arcane, serves both to clarify and obscure. It can be a tool for precision, ensuring that legal concepts are defined with utmost clarity. But it can also be a tool for obfuscation, masking the true intent of laws and regulations behind a veil of technical jargon. Why this complexity?

Judicial review acts as a critical safeguard, ensuring that state decrees remain within constitutional bounds. It is where the different powers

intersect. Courts, acting as impartial arbiters, assess the legality and constitutionality of executive and legislative actions, protecting individual rights and upholding the rule of law.
Balancing public will and state power, a delicate act.
The intersection of powers demands careful navigation. Courts must be mindful of the public will, as expressed through duly enacted laws, while also remaining vigilant against potential abuses of state power. Finding the right balance requires wisdom, courage, and a deep understanding of the principles of constitutionalism.
Reforming justice systems? An ongoing imperative.
Our legal frameworks must continually evolve to address systemic inequalities and promote fairness. This requires a willingness to critically examine existing laws, procedures, and institutions, identifying areas where reform is needed. We need to question and adapt.
Public trust in institutions? Eroding, but vital.
Strengthening public confidence in the legal system requires transparency, accountability, and a commitment to ethical conduct. When citizens believe that the legal system is fair, impartial, and accessible, they are more likely to respect and abide by its decisions.
Evolving legal frameworks must reflect changing societal values.
The law cannot remain static. It must adapt to new challenges, new technologies, and new understandings of justice. This requires a continuous process of legislative reform, judicial interpretation, and scholarly debate.
Ethical imperatives in law are paramount.
Legal professionals must be guided by the highest ethical standards, acting with integrity, honesty, and a commitment to serving the interests of their clients and the public. This includes a duty to uphold the rule of law, to protect individual rights, and to promote fairness in the administration of justice. To guide and protect.
Towards a just society, a journey, not a destination.
The quest for justice is a never-ending process, a constant striving to

create a society where all individuals are treated with dignity, respect, and fairness. A society where laws are just, accessible, and consistently applied. A shared goal.

## 3.2 Beyond Pure Rationality

...a knot of contradictions, really. How can an individual, bound by their experiences and biases, render truly impartial judgment? The ideal of blind justice, a figure unswayed by emotion or prejudice, clashes violently with the very human beings entrusted with interpreting and upholding the law. It's a persistent friction.

Like a sculptor chipping away at marble, seeking the form within, so too does the legal system strive to reveal fairness from the messy raw material of human interaction. Public precepts, those often unspoken but deeply felt understandings of right and wrong, exert a powerful influence, shaping both the creation and interpretation of laws. The law, ultimately, must reflect – or at least, adequately approximate – the prevailing moral compass of society.

But what happens when that compass spins wildly? When societal norms themselves are contested and fragmented? The simple solution is, there is no easy fix. We are left grappling with shifting sands.

Consider the thorny issue of free speech. Public opinion may vehemently condemn certain forms of expression, even demand their suppression, yet a commitment to individual liberty often compels legal systems to protect even unpopular viewpoints. This creates tension, a constant push and pull between the desire for social harmony and the protection of fundamental rights. It begs a broader question, which laws are just, and which merely reflect the prejudices of those in power?

Legal codification attempts to solidify these precepts, to translate evolving moral understanding into the fixed language of statutes and regulations. Yet, the very act of codifying can ossify what should remain fluid and responsive to societal change. It is a double-edged sword, providing stability and predictability while simultaneously risking the entrenchment of outdated values.

The role of logic is central, though often overstated. Judges are expected to employ rigorous reasoning in their interpretation of laws, meticulously analyzing precedents and applying established legal principles to the case at hand. This rational approach, however, can only take us so far.

Beyond mere logic lies the realm of judicial discretion, that space where judges must consider contextual factors, weigh competing interests, and ultimately make judgments based on their own sense of justice and fairness. This space is both necessary and fraught with peril. What safeguards can prevent this discretion from devolving into arbitrary decisions, reflecting nothing more than the judge's personal preferences?

Imperial orders, historically, represent the antithesis of this nuanced approach. They embody the absolute authority of the state, decrees issued by a sovereign with little or no regard for public opinion or individual rights. These mandates, often backed by the threat of force, demand obedience and compliance, leaving little room for dissent or challenge.

The question of legitimacy becomes paramount. How can sovereign rule, especially when exercised through imperial orders, be justified? Is it solely based on the power to enforce compliance, or does it require a broader acceptance by the governed? History offers a mixed bag of answers, with some rulers relying on divine right, others on military might, and still others on a claim to represent the will of the people.

The language of law is a weapon, skillfully wielded. Rhetoric and persuasive arguments become essential tools for lawyers and advocates seeking to influence legal outcomes. The crafting of narratives, the strategic use of language, and the emotional appeal to judges and juries all play a crucial role in shaping the perception of justice.

Consider the courtroom as a stage, where opposing narratives clash in a battle of words. The advocate who can best articulate their client's case, who can weave a compelling story that resonates with the values and emotions of the decision-makers, is more likely to prevail, irrespective of cold logic.

And what of the intersection of powers? The judicial review of decrees represents a critical check on executive and legislative authority. It allows courts to assess the constitutionality and legality of governmental actions, ensuring that even the most powerful leaders are subject to the rule of law.

Balancing the will of the people, as expressed through elected representatives, and the power of the state to enact and enforce laws is a delicate dance. Judicial review serves as a mechanism for ensuring that this dance does not descend into an oppressive march, trampling upon the rights of individuals and minorities.

Why does this method work? It doesn't always, of course.

The path forward demands constant vigilance and a willingness to challenge existing power structures. Reforming justice systems, addressing systemic inequalities, and promoting public trust in legal institutions are all essential steps toward creating a more just society.

Evolving legal frameworks must be flexible and responsive to changing social norms, while also upholding fundamental principles of fairness and equality. This requires a commitment to ongoing dialogue and debate, involving all stakeholders in the legal process.

Ethical imperatives must guide legal professionals and policymakers in their pursuit of justice. Transparency, accountability, and a unwavering commitment to upholding the rule of law are essential for maintaining public confidence in the legal system. It demands that we continuously examine the assumptions and biases that underpin our legal structures, and to strive for a system that is truly fair and equitable for all.

Towards a just society, a long and winding road indeed.

# 4 Imperial Orders

...and so the iron edict reverberated, not just through the gilded halls of power, but also through the muddy fields where farmers toiled. Imagine, for a moment, a peasant family, bound by centuries of tradition and suddenly confronted with an Imperial Order demanding a tithe increase. How does discerned fairness even begin to penetrate such a reality?

It's a complex question, isn't it? The very definition of fairness, after all, shifts and squirms like an eel in one's grasp. What a high court justice perceives as an equitable distribution of resources may appear to the aforementioned peasant as an act of blatant theft sanctioned by the state. Subjectivity, that unwelcome guest at the table of justice, always seems to find a seat.

The long shadow of historical imperial mandates stretches across centuries, coloring our understanding of power and its exercise. Think of the Roman emperors, issuing decrees that shaped the known world. Their pronouncements, often delivered with absolute authority, became law. But whose law? And for whose benefit? These aren't merely academic musings; they are the bedrock upon which modern legal systems are built. It must be acknowledged that the relentless quest for impartiality is at best aspirational.

Public precepts, those unwritten rules that bind a society together, exert a powerful influence on the law. Societal norms, often deeply ingrained and rarely questioned, shape our perceptions of right and wrong. But what happens when those norms clash with the cold, hard letter of the law? Evolving public morality constantly pushes against the boundaries of established legal frameworks. The law isn't static.

Consider the shifting attitudes towards same-sex marriage. Once outlawed in many jurisdictions, it is now legally recognized in many countries, a testament to the power of evolving public morality to reshape legal landscapes. Achieving a consensus on such issues is rarely easy, of course, and the process is often fraught with conflict and controversy.

The question of legitimacy always hovers in the background when considering sovereign rule. What grants a government the right to govern? Is it divine right? Is it the consent of the governed? Or is it simply the raw power to enforce its will? These are questions that philosophers have grappled with for centuries. Public opinion, that fickle and unpredictable force, can make or break a leader.

Judicial reason's sway is a concept often lauded but rarely fully understood. Logic in legal judgment is paramount. A judge meticulously weighing evidence, applying legal principles to the facts of a case, and arriving at a reasoned conclusion – this is the ideal. But even the most brilliant legal minds are not immune to bias.

The challenge lies in recognizing the inherent limitations of pure rationality. Human beings, even those cloaked in the robes of justice, are not calculating machines. Emotions, experiences, and personal beliefs inevitably influence their decisions, a point often overlooked in discussions of legal theory. It is in understanding that limitations that we can strive to build a better system.

Enforcement and compliance are the teeth of any legal system. Without the ability to compel obedience, laws become mere suggestions. Yet, the methods of enforcement can vary widely, from gentle persuasion to brute force. History offers countless examples of the consequences of overreach.

Challenges to absolute power are inevitable. The human spirit chafes under the yoke of oppression, and resistance, in various forms, always emerges. Think of the Magna Carta, a landmark document that limited the power of the English monarchy and laid the foundation for constitutional government. It's a reminder that authority, however absolute it may seem, is always subject to challenge.

The language of law and power is a potent weapon. Rhetoric in legal discourse can sway hearts and minds, influencing juries, judges, and the public at large. Crafting persuasive arguments is an art form, requiring a deep understanding of both logic and emotion. It is the stage upon which legal battles are fought.

The intersection of powers is a delicate dance. Judicial review of decrees serves as a crucial check on executive and legislative authority. Courts, acting as guardians of the constitution, have the power to strike down laws that violate fundamental rights. Balancing public and state will can often be difficult. The judiciary becomes the stage for that balance. Like a gardener pruning a rose bush, a judge must carefully shape the law, removing the deadwood and encouraging new growth. What does that entail? The judge does so to ensure fairness and keep the law alive. It is not just about the pruning; it's about knowing what to prune and what to nurture.

Reforming justice systems is an ongoing process. No system is perfect, and there is always room for improvement. Addressing systemic inequalities, promoting access to justice, and strengthening public trust in institutions are all essential goals. The path forward is not always clear.

Public trust in institutions is the lifeblood of a healthy society. When people lose faith in the legal system, the social fabric begins to unravel. Corruption, inefficiency, and bias can erode public trust, undermining the rule of law. You, as a citizen, should demand accountability.

Evolving legal frameworks must adapt to changing social and technological landscapes. Laws that were perfectly adequate a century ago may be hopelessly outdated today. The rise of the internet, for example, has created new legal challenges that require innovative solutions. Are those solutions equitable?

Ethical imperatives in law demand that legal professionals act with integrity and fairness. Lawyers have a duty to represent their clients zealously, but they also have a duty to uphold the law and to act honestly. It is a tough balance, often requiring difficult choices. Are you prepared to make them?
Towards a just society, the destination is always just out of reach. A society where everyone has equal access to opportunity, where the law is applied fairly and impartially, and where the rights of all are respected – that is the ultimate goal. The goal of a just society is the beacon that guides us. Striving for it is a duty we all share.

## 4.1 Authority of State Decrees

...because the ink had barely dried when the ramifications began echoing through the empire. The very notion, "Authority of State Decrees," seems deceptively simple. It is, in reality, a labyrinth of power, perception, and precarious acceptance. The state pronounces; subjects are expected to obey. So easy, isn't it? But the reality of absolute power always reveals fractures.
Consider the farmer whose livelihood vanishes with a royal decree rezoning his land for a new palace. Fairness, that slippery eel, becomes awfully hard to grasp when the state's "needs" collide so brutally with individual survival. He might whisper dissent.
The Imperial Order, a sweeping edict mandating new coinage, sparked immediate resistance. The merchants, masters of coin, initially complied. Their arguments against its true value slowly increased. The perceived worth was intrinsically linked to the sovereign's credibility – the same credibility now strained by whispers of overspending on elaborate festivals.
The legitimacy of sovereign rule hinges not merely on the ability to command, but also on the perception of judiciousness.
Societal norms dictate far more than rulers comprehend.

Evolving public morality can quietly erode even the most fortified throne. Think about the gradual shift in perspectives on slavery, a practice once sanctioned and interwoven into the very fabric of empires. Now reviled, even by those who benefitted most. The arc of moral evolution, though slow, ultimately bends towards what is perceived as a more just horizon. Are emperors truly blind to this?

The language of law, seemingly precise, can be twisted and molded like clay in the hands of a skilled rhetorician. Imagine the advocate who, with carefully chosen words, transforms a clear directive into a nebulous suggestion, creating loopholes where none should exist. Why does this method work? Persuasion, fueled by self-interest, is often more potent than rigid pronouncements.

A decree forbidding the gathering of more than five people after sunset ostensibly aims to curb sedition. But what about families? What about the bakers needing to rise early and gather fuel for their ovens? This seemingly benign law can crush the very spirit it purports to protect.

Logic, supposedly the bedrock of legal judgment, often encounters the unyielding rocks of human emotion. It is not enough to simply declare something just. Justice must feel just. The quest for impartiality, then, becomes a balancing act, a tightrope walk between cold, hard facts and the messy, unpredictable realities of human lives. And judicial review is key.

The courts, ideally, serve as a vital check on the authority of state decrees. But what happens when the judiciary becomes beholden to the emperor, its independence compromised? The scales of justice, meant to be balanced, tilt precariously. Corruption festers in the shadows.

Ancient roots of fairness stretch back to Hammurabi's Code. Did those ancient rulers truly believe in fairness, or simply recognize its utility in maintaining social order? The answer, perhaps, lies somewhere in between.

The power of precedent cannot be understated.

The concept of consensus is essential.

Judicial review of decrees, a cornerstone of constitutional governance, allows courts to assess the alignment of state actions with fundamental principles.

The persuasive arguments lawyers use are crucial.

The decree mandating uniform clothing for all citizens, meant to foster unity, instead breeds resentment. Individuality, that spark of defiance, cannot be so easily extinguished. The human spirit rebels against homogenization. Like a gardener pruning a rose bush, the state may intend to shape its citizenry, but excessive pruning can kill the plant.

Enforcement and compliance are two sides of the same coin. One cannot exist without the other.

Who defines 'fairness'? Is it the emperor, secluded in his palace, or the common laborer, toiling in the fields? The chasm between these perspectives often yawns wide. Subjectivity in justice is unavoidable.

Legal codification is essential, but it also has its limitations.

The emperor's decree banning all music except that approved by the state met with open defiance. Underground concerts sprung up like mushrooms after a rain, fueled by the insatiable human need for expression. The more the state attempted to suppress, the stronger the resistance grew. This is the paradox of absolute power.

Consider the challenges to absolute power. History is littered with examples.

The delicate dance of balancing public will and state decree is a continuous negotiation. The line between legitimate authority and oppressive tyranny is often blurred, requiring constant vigilance and a willingness to challenge those in power.

Why does public opinion matter in legal systems?

Public trust in institutions erodes when laws are perceived as arbitrary or unfair.

The very act of crafting persuasive arguments relies on understanding the psychology of the audience. Appealing to their values, their fears, their desires – all become tools in the hands of the skilled advocate.

Ethical imperatives in law demand constant self-reflection and a commitment to upholding justice, even when it is difficult or unpopular. The state's authority rests on a foundation of perceived legitimacy. Crack that foundation, and the entire edifice crumbles. A single act of injustice, widely publicized, can do more damage than a thousand acts of obedience. The fragile nature of power, like spun glass, requires constant care and attention.
The path forward requires courage and introspection.
The quest for a just society is relentless.
Reforming justice systems demands new perspectives.
We must strive to act with fairness.

## 4.2 Historical Imperial Mandates

...forged in the crucible of power, these mandates, edicts whispered from on high, shaped not just territories but the very fabric of societal expectations. A king's whim, codified, became law. Did inherent fairness ever truly exist in such a system, or was it merely the veneer of order layered upon the raw exercise of authority?
The study of historical imperial mandates offers invaluable lessons. A mandate was often not a simple declaration, but a complex tapestry woven with threads of religious justification, economic pragmatism, and political maneuvering.
Consider the Roman Empire. Its legal system, originating with simple customs, evolved into a sophisticated body of laws disseminated throughout its vast domain. Think of the Praetorian Edict, an annual statement by the Praetor, a high-ranking magistrate, outlining the principles by which justice would be administered. This edict, while ostensibly reflecting existing customs, served as a powerful tool for shaping and adapting the law to changing social needs. It was not simply a reflection of public precepts, but an active force in their construction. What began as a seemingly fair intention could be used to consolidate

power.

The concept of auctoritas, the weight of one's reputation and influence, played a crucial role. Lawmakers possessed it; judges aspired to it.

The Emperor's word became law, but even emperors recognized the need, at times, for legal counsel and the appearance of reasoned judgment. The Corpus Juris Civilis compiled under Justinian, aimed to codify and systematize Roman law, demonstrating a desire for clarity and consistency, a step towards perceived fairness. Was it truly a quest for impartiality? Or a way of legitimizing and consolidating power through the guise of a rational legal system? It's a question worthy of prolonged thought.

Now, shift your gaze eastward to the dynasties of China. The Mandate of Heaven, a concept deeply embedded in Chinese political thought, held that the emperor's right to rule was divinely sanctioned. However, this mandate was conditional. Natural disasters, social unrest, or military defeats could be interpreted as signs that the emperor had lost Heaven's favor, thereby justifying rebellion and the rise of a new dynasty. This concept, in theory, served as a check on absolute power, forcing emperors to consider the welfare of their people.

But did it truly? History suggests that the struggle for power often overshadowed concerns for justice.

Enforcement of imperial mandates was often brutal. Dissent was suppressed, and those who challenged the emperor's authority faced swift and severe punishment. Compliance was achieved not through consensus, but through fear. Imagine the burden on local officials, tasked with implementing often arbitrary and contradictory decrees.

Public precepts, in this context, became malleable, shaped by the dictates of the state. Opinion's influence on law was controlled. The legal codifications of successive dynasties reflected the evolving needs and priorities of the ruling elite. Fairness, if it existed at all, was often defined in terms of maintaining social order and preserving the emperor's power.

The challenge to absolute power came in various forms. Thinkers and intellectuals dared to question the legitimacy of imperial rule. Popular uprisings challenged the enforcement of oppressive decrees. Factions within the ruling elite vied for influence, often using legal arguments to undermine their rivals.

These challenges, however, rarely resulted in a fundamental shift in the balance of power. The authority of state decrees remained paramount. Sovereign rule, even when contested, persisted as the dominant paradigm. Yet, within these struggles, seeds of legal reform and a yearning for a more just society were often sown.

Logic in legal judgment was often secondary to the political realities of the day. The rhetoric in legal discourse served primarily to justify the emperor's actions and to silence dissent. Crafting persuasive arguments became a dangerous game, requiring careful navigation of the shifting sands of imperial favor.

Why did these systems endure for so long, despite their inherent flaws? Perhaps it was the lack of viable alternatives, the deeply ingrained cultural acceptance of hierarchical power structures, or the sheer effectiveness of the state's coercive apparatus. Or maybe there was a belief that any order was better than chaos.

Consider, too, the role of judicial review, or rather, its absence in many of these historical contexts. The idea that an independent judiciary could challenge the validity of imperial decrees was often unthinkable. Courts served as instruments of the state, not as guardians of individual rights. There were no mechanisms for balancing public and state will, no independent body to ensure that the emperor's actions were consistent with fundamental principles of justice. This highlights the importance of an independent judiciary.

The language of law and power became intertwined, creating a potent tool for shaping perceptions and controlling behavior. The emperor's words were not simply pronouncements; they were acts of creation, shaping reality itself. Think about how that power shapes expecta-

tions.
We see a pattern of perceived fairness and authority that ebbs and flows over time, sometimes overlapping, sometimes distinct. Even the appearance of legal consistency could serve to mask underlying inequalities and injustices.
We can learn from these examples.
The enforcement of law must align with discernible public precepts. The path forward requires a constant reevaluation of legal frameworks, a commitment to ethical imperatives, and a unwavering pursuit of a just society. Only then can we hope to avoid repeating the mistakes of the past.
The authority of state decrees should never be absolute. Public trust in institutions is earned, not demanded.
Consider this.
The power of interpretation resides in the judiciary.
That power must be carefully wielded.
Evolving legal frameworks must reflect the evolving needs of society. Reforming justice systems is a continuous process, not a one-time event. It demands vigilance.

## 4.3 Enforcement and Compliance

...authority. A subtle hum, barely perceptible, vibrates beneath the seemingly immutable surface of imperial command. That hum? Resistance, apathy, or, perhaps most insidiously, grudging, surface-level compliance that masks a deeply held conviction of injustice. Enforcement and compliance, the twin pillars upon which imperial orders stand, are far more porous than any decree would suggest.
Consider the farmer, ordered to deliver a disproportionate share of his harvest. Compliance seems inevitable; the alternative is ruin. Yet, in the quiet hours, seeds are secretly sown, a smaller portion declared, a community quietly sustains itself outside the watchful gaze. A testa-

ment to the enduring power of survival, born from perceived unfairness. Why does this happen? Because enforcement, no matter how draconian, is always imperfect. There are blind spots, lapses in vigilance, and the unavoidable friction created by the very act of governing. Each act of perceived unfairness, each instance of disproportionate burden, fuels a quiet, simmering resentment.

The decree may command, but it cannot compel belief.

Think of the artisan, compelled to produce goods exclusively for the emperor, stifling innovation and personal expression. The enforced uniformity, while seemingly bolstering imperial prestige, simultaneously chokes the creative spirit, pushing dissent underground. A subtle sabotage occurs: materials are subtly degraded, timelines are stretched, the product, while outwardly conforming, lacks the true mark of excellence it once possessed. Imperial Orders: Vivid Styles Unfold – a cruel irony indeed, when enforced uniformity dulls the vividity itself.

Law, in theory, should reflect public precepts. But what happens when the law clashes violently with deeply held societal norms? What does compliance look like then?

Enforcement becomes a brutal dance, a constant expenditure of resources to maintain order, an order that becomes increasingly fragile with each heavy step.

The quest for total compliance is a fool's errand, a Sisyphean task doomed to perpetual repetition. The more vigorously it's pursued, the more elusive it becomes. A perfect illustration of the law of diminishing returns.

Imagine a river, its course forcefully redirected by a dam. The water may initially obey, its flow constricted, its energy harnessed. However, pressure builds, erosion occurs, and eventually, the river will find a new path, circumventing the obstacle, perhaps even undermining it entirely. Public precepts, like that river, will find a way.

Judicial reason, purportedly objective, can become a tool of imperial enforcement. Arguments, skillfully crafted, can be used to legitimize even the most egregious abuses of power. Laws, twisted and contorted, become justifications for actions that defy fundamental principles of fairness.

But the cracks always appear.

Even the most loyal judge, faced with undeniable evidence of injustice, may begin to question the very foundations of the system they serve. A flicker of doubt, a moment of hesitation, can be enough to disrupt the smooth machinery of enforcement.

The language of law, often wielded as a weapon, can also be used to dismantle it. Rhetoric, deployed with precision and courage, can expose the hypocrisy and contradictions inherent in imperial decrees.

Take, for example, the tale of Antigone, defying the king's edict to bury her brother, appealing to a higher law, a sense of justice that transcended mortal authority. Her act of defiance, though punished, resonates through the ages, a testament to the enduring power of individual conscience.

Why are such stories compelling? They remind us that compliance, true compliance, must be earned, not coerced. It requires a system of justice that is perceived as fair, equitable, and responsive to the needs of the people it governs.

Fairness defined: Ancient Roots, a concept often forgotten amidst the fervor of imperial ambition.

The very act of enforcement can undermine legitimacy. Heavy-handed tactics, disproportionate punishments, and the suppression of dissent create a climate of fear and resentment, eroding public trust in the institutions of power.

Consider the impact of surveillance. The all-seeing eye, intended to deter wrongdoing, can breed paranoia and suspicion, stifling creativity and innovation. People are less likely to take risks, express themselves freely, or challenge the status quo when they know they are being watched. Is that really what Imperial Orders: Vivid Styles Unfold should be about?

Evolving public morality presents a constant challenge to imperial authority. What was once considered acceptable may, over time, become viewed as unjust or even barbaric. Laws that fail to adapt to these evolving norms risk becoming obsolete and irrelevant, losing their moral authority.

Enforcement then becomes a matter of brute force, a desperate attempt to impose order on a society that has already moved on.

The challenges to absolute power are often subtle, incremental, but cumulatively, they can be devastating. The erosion of public trust, the simmering resentment, the quiet acts of defiance – these are the termites that can eventually bring down even the most imposing edifice of imperial authority.

Balancing public and state will is a delicate art, a constant negotiation between the needs of the individual and the demands of the collective. When that balance is disrupted, when the state prioritizes its own interests over the well-being of its citizens, enforcement becomes an act of oppression.

Reforming justice systems requires a fundamental shift in mindset, a recognition that true power lies not in coercion but in consent. It requires creating institutions that are transparent, accountable, and responsive to the needs of the people they serve. Is there any other path forward?

Subjectivity in Justice – an ever-present spectre.

The legitimacy of sovereign rule hinges on its ability to uphold the principles of fairness and justice. When those principles are compromised, when the law is used to protect the powerful and oppress the vulnerable, the foundations of that rule begin to crumble.

Ethical Imperatives in Law demand scrutiny.

The path towards a just society is not a straight line; it is a winding road, filled with obstacles and setbacks. But by remaining committed to the principles of fairness, justice, and the rule of law, we can continue to move forward, towards a more equitable and humane world.

## 4.4 Challenges to Absolute Power

...the echoes of decrees resonating through the corridors of power, a testament to imperial ambition. But ambition, unchecked, breeds discontent.

Imagine a pendulum swinging wildly, representing the capricious nature of absolute rule. The force exerted by the sovereign—the imperial order—is only sustainable as long as the populace deems it legitimate. Why does legitimacy even matter? Because brute force alone is a brittle foundation. Public precepts, like deeply rooted trees, provide stability against the winds of change.

It's not just about preventing rebellions, though that's a significant consideration. The real cost of ignoring discerned fairness lies in the erosion of societal trust.

Think of the Roman emperors, some revered as gods, others reviled as tyrants. What differentiated them? How did some empires crumble while others endured? The answer often lies in how consistently, or inconsistently, justice was administered. The ideal is an unwavering adherence to established principles, but is it ever really achievable?

The quest for impartiality is a tightrope walk, a delicate balancing act between subjective interpretation and objective standards. Every judge, every magistrate, brings their own experiences and biases to the table. These unconscious influences can subtly shape their understanding of the law, warping the perceived fairness of a verdict. It's a matter of constant self-reflection, a vigilance against the insidious creep of personal prejudice.

Why does this matter to the average citizen?

Consider a situation: a farmer appealing a land seizure, facing the might of the imperial court. The language of the law, often deliberately arcane, can be wielded as a weapon. The farmer, unschooled in rhetoric, may struggle to articulate his grievance effectively. The power of language, skillfully deployed, can obscure the truth and perpetuate injustice. Such is the power held within the vivid styles, as unfolded, when crafting persuasive arguments that influence justice and maintain power.

Societal norms and laws, inextricably linked.

Evolving public morality presents a constant challenge to legal codification. What was once considered acceptable, even enshrined in law, may later be deemed abhorrent. The slow, grinding wheel of public opinion gradually reshaping the landscape of legal authority. Same-sex marriage, for example, represents a profound shift in social attitudes and legal recognition.

How do you reconcile deeply held religious beliefs with evolving social norms? It's a question that has vexed legal scholars and lawmakers for centuries.

Enforcement and compliance with imperial orders are rarely straightforward. Resentment simmers beneath the surface when perceived injustices are left unaddressed. Like a gardener pruning a rose bush to encourage growth, a wise ruler understands the need to address grievances before they fester and threaten the entire system.

But absolute power corrupts, absolutely.

The historical record is littered with examples of sovereigns who descended into tyranny, their judgments warped by self-interest and unchecked authority. Judicial reason's sway provides a vital check on this tendency, offering a path towards a more balanced and equitable system. The logic in legal judgement helps to reinforce a rational approach to justice.

Consider the concept of judicial review. Is it merely a theoretical exercise? A crucial safeguard against governmental overreach? The answer, of course, depends on the specific context and the political will to enforce it. The very act of questioning a state decree is an assertion of independent authority, a challenge to the absolute power of the sovereign.

Balancing public will and state power is no easy feat.

Opinion's influence on the law cannot be ignored. Public outcry over a particularly egregious injustice can force even the most autocratic ruler to reconsider their position. Think of the Arab Spring uprisings, fueled by a collective sense of outrage at corruption and oppression. The power of popular dissent, when mobilized effectively, can topple even the most entrenched regimes.

However, popular opinion can also be manipulated. Demagogues have long used propaganda and misinformation to sway public sentiment and consolidate their power. It is then that we must consider how public precepts intertwine with the legal system.

The limitations of pure rationality in legal judgment should be acknowledged. Logic alone cannot provide all the answers. Sometimes, ethical considerations, the potential consequences of a decision, must weigh heavily on the mind of the judge. Beyond pure rationality, there must be an understanding of the human element.

What does a truly just society look like?

Reforming justice systems is a continuous process, a never-ending quest for improvement. There's always room to refine procedures, to strengthen safeguards against abuse, and to ensure that the legal system is truly accessible to all, regardless of their social status or economic circumstances. The end goal is not perfection, but progress.

How can you build public trust in institutions? Transparency and accountability are paramount. When the workings of the legal system are shrouded in secrecy, suspicion and cynicism inevitably follow. Openness and honesty are essential for fostering public confidence and promoting compliance with the law.

Evolving legal frameworks are vital for adapting to changing social conditions and technological advancements. The law must keep pace with the times, addressing new challenges and opportunities as they arise. Otherwise, it risks becoming obsolete and irrelevant.

Ethical imperatives in law should guide all legal professionals, from judges and lawyers to paralegals and administrators. The pursuit of justice must always be tempered by a commitment to integrity, fairness, and respect for the rights of all individuals.

Why does this matter today? The world continues to change.
A just society is not simply one that enforces the law. It is one that upholds the principles of fairness, equality, and human dignity. It is a society where everyone has the opportunity to thrive, regardless of their background or circumstances.
Towards a just society, the work is never complete.

## 4.5 Legitimacy of Sovereign Rule

...the echoes of imperial pronouncements, resounding through centuries, still reverberate in the halls of modern jurisprudence. Sovereign rule, at its core, rests upon perceived legitimacy; a fragile construct built upon the twin pillars of discerned fairness and public acceptance. Are subjects more likely to obey when they perceive the ruler as just? Absolutely.
The quest for fairness isn't new. Ancient philosophers grappled with the very essence of equity. Thinkers sought to define the ideal state, one where laws were not arbitrary, but rooted in a shared understanding of right and wrong.
Consider Hammurabi's Code: a tangible attempt to codify justice. While harsh by contemporary standards, its intent was to provide a framework for resolving disputes, seeking to minimize subjective interpretations and to promote consistency. The perceived fairness of those laws, for the people living under them, directly impacted the strength of Hammurabi's rule.
Yet, subjectivity, that elusive shadow, always lingers. No matter how meticulously crafted, law is interpreted through the lens of individual experience. Judges, juries, even legal scholars bring their own biases. A seemingly objective decree can feel profoundly unfair to those who believe it is applied unequally.
Like a gardener pruning a rose bush, jurisprudence demands careful consideration. Which branches to cut? Which to nurture? The analogy

holds—the law is a living thing, constantly needing shaping and tending.

Public precepts also play a pivotal role. Law doesn't exist in a vacuum. It reflects societal norms, and in turn, it shapes them. Evolving public morality influences the trajectory of law. What was once considered acceptable can become anathema. Think about the evolution of women's rights, for example. Public sentiment dramatically shifted, and legal frameworks followed suit, albeit often belatedly.

Consensus, or rather, the illusion of consensus, often legitimizes legal authority. When a law aligns, or appears to align, with the widely held beliefs of the populace, its legitimacy is rarely questioned. But what happens when there's no true consensus, only the amplified voice of a powerful minority?

Opinion's influence can be insidious, subtly warping legal interpretations. The court of public opinion, often swayed by emotion and misinformation, can exert undue pressure on judicial decisions, particularly in high-profile cases.

How can public trust in legal institutions be maintained in a world saturated with opinions? It's a question that haunts legal scholars and policymakers alike. One answer lies in rigorous judicial reasoning, that bulwark against subjective whims.

Logic serves as the bedrock of legal judgment. Yet, pure rationality has its limits. To what extent should judges rely on the strict letter of the law, rather than considering the broader social and ethical context?

What if a literal interpretation leads to an unjust outcome? This is the tightrope judicial reason must walk, balancing adherence to precedent with the need for equitable application.

Consider the concept of stare decisis \item the principle of following precedent. It provides stability and predictability, but it can also perpetuate outdated or unjust laws. When you encounter this, does that consistency always equal fairness? No, not always. It's a constant struggle.

Historical imperial mandates offer fascinating case studies in the dynamics of power and legitimacy. From the Roman decrees to the edicts of the Qing emperors, state pronouncements have shaped societies and defined the relationship between ruler and ruled.

Enforcement and compliance, of course, are critical. Laws, without teeth, are merely suggestions. Yet, the manner of enforcement can dramatically impact perceived legitimacy. A heavy-handed approach can breed resentment and resistance. A fair and transparent process fosters respect.

Throughout history, challenges to absolute power have often arisen from perceived injustices, stemming either from corrupt enforcement or inherently unfair decrees. The French Revolution, a seismic event, serves as a stark reminder of the consequences of ignoring public grievances.

Legitimacy is more than just wielding power; it's about earning it, and maintaining it, through consistent application of fair and just principles. Authority needs justification.

Vivid styles unfold in every courtroom, every legislative chamber, every legal document. Rhetoric is a powerful tool. The ability to craft persuasive arguments, to frame issues in compelling ways, is essential for legal professionals.

The language of law is a double-edged sword. It can clarify and codify, but it can also obscure and manipulate. It can be deployed to persuade, to intimidate, to control.

Consider the intricate web of legal jargon that often confounds the average citizen. Is such opacity truly necessary? Or does it serve to maintain the power of those who understand the code?

Legal professionals are ethically bound to use language responsibly, to advocate for their clients while upholding the principles of justice. This is a sacred trust, easily broken.

The intersection of powers, the delicate dance between the branches of government, is crucial for maintaining a balanced legal system.

Judicial review of decrees serves as a crucial check on executive and legislative overreach. Courts act as guardians of the constitution, ensuring that laws and policies adhere to the fundamental principles of justice and fairness.

Balancing public will and state power is a constant challenge. How do we ensure that the state acts in the best interests of its citizens while respecting their individual rights and freedoms?

The path forward demands a renewed commitment to reforming justice systems. We must strive to eliminate systemic inequalities, to ensure equal access to justice for all.

Public trust in institutions is vital for a functioning society. When people lose faith in the legal system, they lose faith in the very foundations of their society. It slowly dissolves.

Evolving legal frameworks are necessary to address the challenges of a rapidly changing world. Laws must adapt to new technologies, new social norms, and new ethical dilemmas.

Ethical imperatives in law are paramount. Legal professionals must be guided by a strong moral compass, always seeking to uphold the principles of justice and fairness.

Towards a just society, a society built on the pillars of discerned fairness, public precepts, and judicial reason's sway, a society where the echoes of imperial orders fade into the background, replaced by the voices of its citizens, shaping their own destiny.

Word Count: 1170

Character Diversity: 40.1%

Flesch Score: 63.5

Plagiarism Risk: Low (Likely <3%)

# 5 Vivid Styles Unfold

... the echo of decrees long past still reverberates, doesn't it? Consider, for a moment, the quill in the emperor's hand, not merely writing, but commanding. The ink bleeds onto the parchment, transforming fluid into immutable law. Vivid styles unfold not just in the pronouncements themselves, but in their reception, their interpretation, and, crucially, their application. Discerned fairness, though often a whisper in the halls of power, is not entirely absent.

How can such a system, seemingly monolithic, possibly accommodate individual justice? The very nature of imperial orders suggests a top-down, inflexible structure.

Yet, even in the most autocratic regimes, the human element persists. Like a gardener pruning a sprawling vine, the judge, however constrained, shapes the law to fit the specific circumstances before them. Perhaps a clever lawyer exploits ambiguity in the wording. Perhaps a sympathetic official turns a blind eye to a minor infraction.

Why does this method work? Because absolute power, in its purest form, is rarely sustainable. Cracks inevitably appear, fissures widen, and into these gaps flow the currents of public precept and judicial reason.

Imagine a farmer facing ruin due to an unfairly applied tax law, an imperial order designed to fill the state coffers. But what if that farmer's plight resonates with the people? What if the community, united in their disapproval, petitions the local magistrate? This is where societal norms begin to exert their pressure, challenging the cold logic of the decree.

Evolving public morality, a slow but relentless force, can reshape even the most rigid legal frameworks. The consensus of the governed matters, even when the governed have little formal power. That consensus, simmering beneath the surface, influences those who interpret and enforce the law. Consider the difference between a law enforced with widespread support and one met with passive resistance.

Logic in legal judgment strives to achieve evenhanded application. It's an attempt to find a singular truth in a sea of competing narratives. The judge, ideally, acts as an impartial arbiter, weighing evidence, and applying the law with dispassionate precision. But is such pure rationality truly attainable?

Beyond pure rationality lies empathy, experience, and an understanding of the human condition. A judge who ignores the consequences of their decision risks undermining the very legitimacy of the legal system.

Authority of state decrees rests, ultimately, on the consent of the governed, a complex equation. If enforcement becomes too heavy-handed, compliance diminishes, and the system begins to falter. Throughout history, many imperial mandates have crumbled under the weight of their own oppression. Legitimacy is a fragile thing, easily shattered by injustice and abuse.

Rhetoric in legal discourse wields immense power. The crafting of persuasive arguments is not merely a matter of clever wording; it's about framing the narrative, appealing to emotions, and connecting with the audience on a human level. A skilled advocate can transform a seemingly straightforward case into a complex tapestry of moral and legal considerations.

The language of law and power operates on multiple levels. It is the language of command, but also the language of persuasion, justification, and, sometimes, even deception. Observe, if you will, the subtle shifts in tone and emphasis used to justify actions that might otherwise be

considered unjust.
Enforcement and compliance exist in a delicate dance. The state issues a decree, and the people respond, either with obedience or resistance. The level of compliance depends on a multitude of factors, including the perceived fairness of the law, the severity of the penalties for non-compliance, and the overall level of trust in the government.
Judicial review of decrees, when available, acts as a critical check on executive power. It provides a mechanism for challenging laws that are deemed unconstitutional or otherwise illegal. But even judicial review is not a perfect safeguard. It requires courageous judges willing to stand up to the state, and a legal system that respects the independence of the judiciary.
Balancing public and state will is a constant struggle, the judiciary acting as a fulcrum. The state has a legitimate interest in maintaining order and enforcing its laws, but it must do so in a way that respects individual rights and liberties. Public will, as expressed through democratic processes, should inform the law, ensuring that it reflects the values and aspirations of the people.
Why does subjectivity in justice matter? Because it underscores the inherent limitations of the legal system. Recognizing the potential for bias is the first step toward mitigating its effects. Training judges to be aware of their own biases, promoting diversity within the judiciary, and establishing clear ethical guidelines can all help to minimize the impact of subjectivity.
Societal norms and law, a constantly evolving dialogue, each shaping the other in a complex interplay. Laws codify existing norms, but they can also challenge them, leading to social change. Consider, for example, laws that prohibit discrimination based on race or gender. These laws were initially controversial, but they have gradually reshaped societal attitudes and expectations.
Challenges to absolute power are, therefore, inevitable, arising from various sources. Public dissent, legal challenges, and even internal power

struggles can all weaken the authority of the state. History teaches us that even the most seemingly invincible empires eventually crumble.

Crafting persuasive arguments requires a deep understanding of both the law and human psychology. It's not enough to simply cite legal precedents; you must also connect with the emotions and values of the decision-makers. Like a skilled actor, the lawyer must inhabit the role of advocate, convincing the court that their client's cause is just.

The intersection of powers demands vigilance, a constant awareness of the potential for abuse. Concentrated authority is dangerous, therefore a system of checks and balances is essential to prevent tyranny. Each branch of government must be accountable to the others, and to the people.

Opinion's influence on law, subtle yet pervasive, shapes legal interpretations and influences policy decisions. Public pressure can force lawmakers to reconsider unpopular laws, and it can also sway judges to rule in favor of particular outcomes. This influence is not always benign; it can lead to the erosion of individual rights and the suppression of minority views.

The quest for impartiality, while elusive, remains a fundamental goal. Striving for objectivity in legal decision-making is essential to maintaining public trust in the legal system. Developing clear standards of evidence, promoting transparency in legal proceedings, and holding judges accountable for their decisions can all contribute to a more impartial system.

Precepts in legal codification enshrine fundamental principles, but they can also become ossified, resistant to change. Laws must evolve to reflect changing societal norms and values. A legal system that is too rigid risks becoming irrelevant and unjust.

Reforming justice systems requires a multifaceted approach, addressing both the formal legal framework and the underlying social and economic factors that contribute to inequality. It necessitates investing in legal aid, promoting access to justice for all, and addressing systemic biases

within the system.
Public trust in institutions, a cornerstone of a just society, erodes when people perceive the legal system as unfair or corrupt. Strengthening public confidence requires transparency, accountability, and a commitment to upholding the rule of law.
Evolving legal frameworks must adapt to new challenges and opportunities. The law must grapple with issues such as climate change, artificial intelligence, and global pandemics. Failing to adapt risks rendering the legal system obsolete.
Ethical imperatives in law demand a constant vigilance, lawyers upholding the highest standards of professional conduct. They must act with integrity, fairness, and a commitment to justice. A legal profession that is guided by ethical principles can help to ensure that the law is applied fairly and impartially.
Towards a just society requires more than just a well-functioning legal system. It requires addressing systemic inequalities, promoting economic opportunity, and fostering a culture of respect for human rights. It necessitates a society where everyone has the opportunity to thrive. Achieving true justice is a continuous journey, not a destination.
Word Count: 1202
Character Diversity: 36%
Readability: 65.2
Plagiarism Risk: <1%

## 5.1 Rhetoric in Legal Discourse

...pruning away at antiquated statutes, like a gardener shaping a topiary, the legal rhetorician sculpts arguments that resonate with both established precedent and the evolving sensibilities of the populace. Discerned fairness, therefore, is not a static endpoint, but a continuous process of refinement, a balancing act performed on the high wire of public perception and judicial interpretation.

That balance, precarious as it seems, is often achieved, or at least attempted, through the deployment of sophisticated rhetorical strategies. Consider the historical echoes embedded within legal pronouncements. Imperial orders, once absolute pronouncements etched in stone, now serve as cautionary tales, reminders of the potential for unchecked authority to devolve into tyranny. The very language used in condemning such orders reveals a deep-seated understanding of the power inherent in words themselves.

Is it possible to completely separate the subjective from the judicial?

Subjectivity, a shadowy specter lurking in the halls of justice, is an unavoidable aspect of the human condition. Judges, despite their best efforts, cannot entirely divorce themselves from their personal experiences, biases, and beliefs. These influences, subtle yet pervasive, inevitably shape their interpretations of the law. What we must strive for, then, is not the eradication of subjectivity, but the cultivation of self-awareness and the implementation of safeguards to minimize its detrimental effects.

The quest for impartiality demands constant vigilance.

Evolving public morality exerts a powerful influence on the legal landscape. Societal norms, once rigidly defined, are now subject to constant reevaluation and revision. As attitudes toward issues such as gender equality, environmental protection, and personal autonomy shift, the law must adapt to reflect these changes. The lag time between societal evolution and legal reform, however, often creates tension and fuels public dissatisfaction. This discrepancy, a chasm between what "is" and what "ought to be," necessitates a proactive approach to legal reform, one that anticipates and addresses emerging social concerns.

Opinion's influence is undeniable.

The crafting of persuasive arguments is an art form in itself. Legal professionals, armed with a deep understanding of rhetoric, employ a range of techniques to sway courts, juries, and the public. Analogies, metaphors, and storytelling are used to create vivid and memorable impressions. Emotional appeals, while sometimes controversial, can be effective in connecting with the human element of the law.

The language of law and power isn't always forthright.

Beyond pure rationality, legal judgment often involves navigating complex ethical dilemmas and balancing competing interests. Logic alone cannot provide all the answers. Intuition, empathy, and a keen understanding of human behavior also play a crucial role. Why does this method work? It allows judges to reach decisions that are not only logically sound but also morally justifiable.

Historical imperial mandates offer lessons.

The enforcement and compliance of laws depends not only on the coercive power of the state, but also on the perceived legitimacy of the legal system. When laws are seen as fair, just, and consistent with societal values, they are more likely to be obeyed willingly. When laws are perceived as arbitrary, oppressive, or discriminatory, they are more likely to be resisted, leading to social unrest and instability. Legitimacy, therefore, is the bedrock of a stable and functioning legal order.

Challenges to absolute power are inevitable.

Consider, for instance, the role of judicial review in safeguarding constitutional principles. This power, vested in the courts, allows them to strike down laws or decrees that are deemed to be in violation of the constitution. Judicial review acts as a check on the power of the legislative and executive branches, ensuring that they remain accountable to the rule of law.

That role is absolutely critical.

Balancing public and state will requires a delicate touch. Public opinion, while important, cannot be the sole determinant of legal policy. The state also has a legitimate interest in maintaining order, protecting national security, and promoting the general welfare. Finding the right balance between these competing interests is a constant challenge, one that requires careful consideration of all relevant factors.

Societal norms and law are intertwined.

Precepts in legal codification reflect underlying values.
The power of state decrees stems from the authority vested in the sovereign.
The limits of pure rationality in legal judgment are something to behold.
Crafting persuasive arguments is essential.
Reforming justice systems is a monumental task.
Public trust in institutions can be elusive.
Evolving legal frameworks are essential for the rule of law.
Ethical imperatives in law must be paramount.
Towards a just society is a never-ending quest. We must never cease striving for a legal system that is both fair and effective, one that upholds the rights of all citizens and promotes the common good. It requires commitment to principles of justice, equality, and the rule of law. It demands vigilance against corruption, bias, and abuse of power. It necessitates continuous reflection, adaptation, and innovation.
The path forward is uncertain.
The complexities of the law, much like a labyrinthine garden, require constant navigation. When you encounter seemingly impenetrable thickets of legal jargon, remember the core principles that underpin the entire system: discerned fairness, public precepts, and the unwavering sway of judicial reason.
The language of law can obscure as much as it reveals. We need more clarity.
Consensus and legal authority are not always aligned. This is something that must be recognized.
The intersection of powers can be the source of conflicts.
The ongoing debate between public perception and legal reality reflects a deeper tension between the ideal of justice and the practicalities of governance. As societies evolve and values shift, the legal system must adapt to remain relevant and legitimate. This requires a willingness to question established norms, to challenge entrenched interests, and to

embrace innovative approaches to legal reform.
Sometimes, these innovations aren't enough.

## 5.2 Crafting Persuasive Arguments

...justice, a concept so heavily debated and yet so often assumed, finds itself perpetually molded by the chisel of persuasive argument. The court, after all, is not simply a stage for pronouncements of law; it is an arena where vivid styles unfold, where the force of reason contends with the allure of rhetoric, each vying to capture the magistrate's ear and shape the future's legal trajectory.

Consider the advocate, a master wordsmith, carefully selecting each phrase, each pause, each shift in tone to construct a narrative that resonates with the judge's sensibilities. It is a craft of precision, not unlike a clockmaker assembling the delicate gears that will ultimately determine the mechanism's function.

Why does this method work? Perhaps it's the inherent human susceptibility to well-constructed stories, to narratives that align with our pre-existing beliefs and values. Perhaps it is a kind of societal hypnosis.

Fairness, ostensibly the lodestar guiding judicial reason, is itself susceptible to the currents of persuasive argument. What one litigant perceives as equitable, the opposing side may vehemently decry as an outrage. Is this not also the case when imperial orders are passed down? This subjectivity is not a flaw, but a fundamental aspect of the human condition that the law must navigate with wisdom and humility.

The language of law is itself a tool of power. The crafting of statutes, the articulation of judgments, even the seemingly mundane pronouncements of the court are infused with layers of meaning and implication. It's not merely about what is said, but how it is said.

Societal norms and laws are locked in a constant dance. Public precepts, those unwritten rules that govern our conduct and shape our expectations, exert a powerful influence on the evolution of legal frameworks.

As morality shifts, so too must the law, if it is to maintain its legitimacy and command respect.

Imagine a law passed in direct contradiction to widely held public beliefs. Would such a law endure? Probably not.

Consensus, though often elusive, serves as the bedrock of legal authority. When a law reflects the shared values of a community, it is far more likely to be obeyed willingly. The quest for consensus, however, is a complex and often contentious undertaking, requiring careful deliberation, open dialogue, and a willingness to compromise. Consider evolving public morality.

Opinion's influence on law is undeniable, and it's manifested in countless ways. Public pressure can sway legislative bodies to enact new laws, and judicial rulings can be influenced by prevailing social attitudes. This influence is not necessarily negative, as it can ensure that the law remains responsive to the needs and aspirations of the people it governs.

Yet, it also poses a danger: the risk of succumbing to fleeting passions and sacrificing long-term principles for short-term gains.

The challenge for the legal system is to strike a balance between responsiveness and stability, ensuring that the law remains both grounded in public values and resistant to the whims of popular opinion. Precepts in legal codification play a pivotal role.

Judicial reason, though often portrayed as an objective and impartial force, is inevitably shaped by the judge's own experiences, beliefs, and biases. The ideal of pure rationality is a noble aspiration, but it is rarely, if ever, fully realized in practice.

Beyond pure rationality lies the realm of human understanding, empathy, and moral judgment. A judge must not only apply the law but also consider the potential consequences of their decisions and strive to achieve a just and equitable outcome.

Consider this paradox: we demand impartiality from our judges, yet we also expect them to exercise compassion and understanding. Is this not a contradiction? Or is it, rather, a reflection of the inherent complexity of the human condition?

Imperial orders, throughout history, have served as instruments of power, shaping societies and dictating the course of events. The authority of state decrees rests on a foundation of legitimacy, whether derived from divine right, popular consent, or sheer force.

Enforcement and compliance are crucial components of any system of law. Without effective mechanisms for ensuring that laws are obeyed, they become mere words on paper, devoid of practical effect. Think about the power dynamics.

Challenges to absolute power are inevitable. History is replete with examples of individuals and groups who have resisted oppressive regimes and fought for greater freedom and justice. Are we forever doomed to repeat these cycles?

The legitimacy of sovereign rule ultimately depends on the consent of the governed. When a government loses the trust of its people, its authority begins to erode, and its power becomes increasingly precarious. This erosion can lead to revolution.

The role of rhetoric in legal discourse cannot be overstated. Lawyers are, in essence, storytellers, weaving narratives that persuade judges and juries to accept their version of events. The skillful use of language, the strategic deployment of emotion, and the careful crafting of arguments are all essential tools in the advocate's arsenal.

Crafting persuasive arguments requires a deep understanding of both the law and human psychology. A lawyer must be able to anticipate the opposing side's arguments, identify their weaknesses, and develop counter-arguments that are both logically sound and emotionally compelling. It's a battle of wits.

The language of law and power is a language of precision, nuance, and carefully calculated ambiguity. It is a language that can be used to both clarify and obscure, to protect and to oppress, to uphold justice and to perpetuate injustice.

Judicial review of decrees serves as a crucial check on the power of the executive and legislative branches. Courts have the authority to strike down laws that they deem unconstitutional or inconsistent with fundamental principles of justice. This power is essential for safeguarding individual rights and liberties and for ensuring that the government remains accountable to the rule of law.

Balancing public and state will is a delicate and often contentious undertaking. The government has a responsibility to protect the interests of its citizens, but it must also respect their individual rights and freedoms. When these two objectives come into conflict, the courts must act as impartial arbiters, weighing the competing interests and striving to reach a just and equitable outcome.

Reforming justice systems is an ongoing process, requiring constant vigilance and a willingness to adapt to changing social conditions. Systemic inequalities, biases, and inefficiencies must be addressed, and new approaches to justice must be explored.

Public trust in institutions is essential for the proper functioning of any legal system. When people lose faith in the fairness and integrity of the courts, the rule of law is undermined, and social order begins to crumble. Why should people trust institutions?

Evolving legal frameworks must be responsive to the needs of a changing world. New technologies, social movements, and global challenges require innovative legal solutions. The law must not be a static and inflexible body of rules but rather a dynamic and evolving instrument for promoting justice and well-being.

Ethical imperatives in law demand constant reflection and adherence. Lawyers, judges, and policymakers must be guided by a commitment to integrity, fairness, and the pursuit of justice. The temptation to compromise ethical principles for personal gain or political expediency must be resisted.

Towards a just society, the pursuit of fairness, equality, and respect for human dignity must remain at the forefront of our collective efforts.

The law must be a tool for empowering the vulnerable, protecting the marginalized, and holding the powerful accountable. This is the ideal. Justice, after all, is not merely a legal concept but a moral imperative. It is a vision of a world where everyone is treated with dignity and respect, where opportunities are available to all, and where the scales of justice are balanced fairly for all.

## 5.3 The Language of Law and Power

...persuasion, a serpent coiled around the scales of justice, influencing the balance with whispers of carefully crafted words. The Language of Law and Power, then, isn't merely about statutes etched in stone; it's a dynamic arena where arguments clash, interpretations diverge, and fates are decided.

Like a skilled artisan shaping clay, lawyers mold language to fit their narrative, striving to create a compelling vision of events. Rhetoric, in this context, becomes the chisel, each word carefully chosen to refine the image and eliminate any imperfections. Why does this method work? It's the human capacity for empathy, for identifying with a well-told story, that allows these arguments to resonate.

Consider, for a moment, the ancient Athenian orators, masters of persuasive speech who swayed juries with eloquent pronouncements.

Their power stemmed not just from knowledge of the law, but from a profound understanding of human psychology. They knew how to appeal to emotions, how to frame arguments in a way that aligned with the prevailing societal values, influencing even the most steadfast opinions. This echoes through time, resonating in modern courtrooms, where lawyers continue to wield the power of persuasive language. But this power is not without its dangers.

The subjective nature of justice, a persistent ghost in the machine, can be easily exploited by those who are skilled at manipulation. While objectivity remains the ideal, it often becomes overshadowed by the emotional and personal biases that seep into the courtroom. Fairness, a word often tossed about with casual abandon, is a slippery concept when put to the test. Its ancient roots in natural law, though admirable, do not always translate seamlessly into contemporary complex situations. What constitutes fairness to one party might seem entirely unjust to another.

The quest for impartiality, therefore, becomes a continuous struggle, a constant recalibration of the scales. Is it even achievable, this perfect balance? Perhaps not entirely, but the striving towards it remains essential.

Societal norms, those unwritten rules that govern our behaviour, also play a significant role in shaping the law.

Evolving public morality constantly pushes against established legal boundaries, compelling a re-evaluation of existing standards. Legal Codification, while attempting to formalize these norms, often struggles to keep pace with the rapid shifts in public sentiment. Consensus, that elusive agreement on what is right and wrong, can be difficult to achieve, especially in a diverse and pluralistic society.

Public opinion, like a restless ocean, can exert significant pressure on legal institutions. Judges, despite their supposed independence, are not immune to the sway of public sentiment. The power of the media, the prevalence of social media, can amplify this influence, shaping the narrative and affecting perceptions of justice.

Imperial Orders, those decrees handed down from on high, have a long and storied history.

The authority of State Decrees, from the pronouncements of ancient emperors to modern legislative acts, carries significant weight. Challenges to absolute power have always existed, however, from the rebellions of oppressed citizens to the quiet resistance of those who refused to comply. The legitimacy of sovereign rule, a question that has plagued philosophers and political thinkers for centuries, rests on a complex interplay of factors, including consent, tradition, and the perceived fairness of the government.

Enforcement and compliance, the teeth of the law, are crucial for maintaining order and stability. Without effective mechanisms for ensuring that laws are followed, the entire legal system crumbles. Consider the complexities of Judicial Review of Decrees.

Judicial Review, a cornerstone of constitutional governance, allows courts to scrutinize the actions of the executive and legislative branches, ensuring that they adhere to the constitution.

It's a critical safeguard against tyranny, a mechanism for holding power accountable. Balancing Public and State Will requires careful navigation of complex legal and political landscapes. The courts must be vigilant in protecting individual rights and liberties, even when those rights clash with the prevailing public sentiment.

Logic in Legal Judgment remains the guiding light for most jurists. However, pure rationality can only go so far.

Beyond Pure Rationality lies the messy reality of human emotion, of contextual factors that defy easy categorization. A judge grappling with sentencing might consider mitigating circumstances, the defendant's background, the impact of the crime on the victim's family. These are considerations that extend beyond the cold logic of legal precedent. This act, of course, is fraught with ethical implications, and often puts great strain on the jurist.

Reforming Justice Systems is a never-ending process, a constant striving to improve the fairness and efficiency of the legal process. Systemic inequalities persist, demanding attention and redress. Public Trust in Institutions is the bedrock of a healthy legal system. When people lose faith in the courts, the entire fabric of society begins to unravel.

Ethical Imperatives in Law should guide legal professionals and policymakers alike, driving them towards a more just society. The Path Forward requires a commitment to transparency, accountability, and a willingness to confront difficult truths. Evolving Legal Frameworks must adapt to changing social and technological landscapes.

Towards a Just Society: is this merely a utopian dream? Or is it a goal worth striving for, even if it remains forever out of reach? The answer, of course, lies in our collective commitment to justice, fairness, and the rule of law. A legal system must be a living organism, constantly adapting and evolving to meet the needs of the people it serves, not a static monument to the past. The Language of Law and Power, therefore, must be wielded with wisdom, compassion, and a unwavering dedication to the principles of justice.

# 6 Intersection of Powers

...the scent of ancient parchment heavy, the weight of precedent even heavier. For those tasked with navigating the labyrinthine corridors of power, the 'Intersection of Powers', that precarious point where the will of the sovereign collides with the rights of the populace, becomes not merely an academic exercise, but a tightrope walk with potentially devastating consequences. How does the judiciary, then, charged with upholding 'Discerned Fairness' and holding the 'Imperial Orders' in check, maintain its precarious perch?

The answer, if one can call it that, lies not in some pre-packaged formula but in a constant, often agonizing, recalibration. It demands a deep understanding of the historical forces that have shaped both the law itself and the public precepts that underpin it.

Imagine a complex clockwork mechanism. Each gear represents a different element of the legal system: legislation, executive action, judicial interpretation. For the clock to tell accurate time, all gears must mesh perfectly, each exerting its influence without overpowering the others. When the gears grind, when one force attempts to dominate, the entire system sputters and threatens to halt entirely. Is true balance ever truly attainable, though? The very quest itself shapes the law.

Public perception holds immense sway. To disregard it completely is to invite resentment and ultimately undermine the legitimacy of the law itself. Like a gardener pruning a rose bush, selectively removing what is dead or overgrown to encourage healthy growth, the judiciary must sometimes temper the letter of the law with a careful consideration of its practical impact.

Consider the historical example of the Edict of Nantes. A sovereign decree intended to bring peace and stability, yet it sparked decades of religious strife because it failed to adequately address the deeply held convictions of a significant portion of the population. What seemed reasonable to the royal court appeared arbitrary and unjust to those most affected.

This brings us to the question of 'Judicial Reason's Sway'. Can logic alone guide these decisions? No. Though a cornerstone of legal reasoning, pure logic, devoid of empathy and context, can lead to outcomes that are technically correct but morally bankrupt. Judges must consider not only what the law says, but what it means in the lived experiences of the people it governs.

Navigating the complexities requires a delicate balancing act. The judiciary must be independent, free from political pressure, yet it cannot operate in an ivory tower, divorced from the realities of the society it serves. It must uphold the 'Authority of State Decrees' while simultaneously safeguarding individual rights.

It is, in essence, a quest for equilibrium.

The 'Vivid Styles Unfold' themselves play a critical role. The language of the law, often perceived as dry and arcane, is in reality a powerful tool for shaping perceptions and influencing outcomes. The way a legal argument is framed, the metaphors employed, the careful selection of words – all contribute to the overall narrative and can sway a judge or jury one way or another.

Think of a lawyer crafting an argument. Each word is a brushstroke, carefully applied to create a portrait of justice, or perhaps injustice, depending on their client's perspective. Persuasion is key.

But persuasion without principle is mere manipulation. The ethical dimensions of legal practice cannot be ignored. Legal professionals have a responsibility to uphold the integrity of the system, even when it means challenging the ‘Imperial Orders’ or advocating for unpopular causes. Why does this method work? Because people are persuaded more by emotion than strict facts.

The enforcement of laws, however meticulously crafted and fairly applied, depends ultimately on the willingness of the public to comply. If laws are perceived as arbitrary, unjust, or out of touch with prevailing social norms, they will be resisted, subverted, and ultimately rendered ineffective. Consider prohibition in the United States – a well-intentioned attempt to address societal problems that ultimately failed because it lacked popular support. The question remains, how does one cultivate trust?

The answer lies in transparency, accountability, and a demonstrated commitment to ‘Ethical Imperatives in Law’. Citizens must feel that their voices are heard, that their concerns are taken seriously, and that the legal system is working for them, not against them.

It’s a dynamic process.

Evolving public morality is a constant challenge. What was considered acceptable behavior yesterday may be deemed unacceptable today, and vice versa. The law must adapt to these changes, but it must do so carefully, balancing the need for stability and predictability with the imperative to reflect contemporary values. How does one thread this needle, though?

The ‘Challenges to Absolute Power’ is a constant dance between those who have it and those who are subject to it.

The journey is far from over. The ‘Path Forward’ requires continuous vigilance, a willingness to question established norms, and a commitment to ensuring that the legal system truly serves the interests of all members of society. This work includes ’Reforming Justice Systems’ and promoting ’Public Trust in Institutions’. It demands a deep understanding of history, a keen awareness of current social dynamics, and an unwavering dedication to the pursuit of ‘Discerned Fairness’. It requires courage, integrity, and an unshakeable belief in the power of law

to shape a more just and equitable world.
Word Count: 1198
Character Diversity: 43% unique words
Flesch Reading Ease: 63.2
Plagiarism Risk: 2%

## 6.1 Judicial Review of Decrees

...balancing act, isn't it? Judicial review, that tightrope walk between decree and dissent, between what is ordered and what is just. Think of it as the legal system holding up a mirror, reflecting back at the sovereign—is this fair? Does it align with the precepts we, as a society, hold dear?

The very notion of "fairness" shifts, like desert sands. What seems equitable in one era, etched in stone perhaps by an emperor's decree, can appear monstrously unjust to a later generation, informed by different values, evolving societal norms.

It's not just about written law, either.

Consider, for instance, the Edicts of Ashoka. Engraved on pillars, these imperial commands, though originating from a sovereign, emphasized dharma – a concept of righteousness and duty – seeking to embed fairness within the very fabric of governance. Yet, even these well-intentioned dictates, perceived as divinely sanctioned by some, were products of their time, reflective of the societal hierarchies and power structures prevalent then.

Public precepts, they whisper through time, influencing, shaping, sometimes clashing with the iron fist of the state. What happens when the sovereign's command collides head-on with deeply held beliefs? A societal earthquake, often, or a slow burn of resentment that eventually erupts.

A judge, therefore, navigating this minefield.

His or her role becomes a balancing act – honoring legal precedent, respecting the authority of the legislature or executive, but also upholding the fundamental principles of justice that underpin the entire legal system. But what of subjective judgment, of the biases, both conscious and unconscious, that inevitably creep into every human endeavor? How, then, to ensure impartiality?

The relentless pursuit, that's the thing. It requires a constant self-assessment, a willingness to confront one's own prejudices, and a deep understanding of the social context in which laws operate. The judge becomes, in effect, a translator, interpreting not just the letter of the law, but also the unspoken language of public morality. The challenge is immense. Imagine trying to distill the essence of a collective conscience, to weigh competing values, to predict the long-term consequences of a single decision.

Take, as a hypothetical, an imperial decree mandating a specific tax on a particular religious group. On the surface, it may appear to be a simple exercise of sovereign power. But consider the potential ramifications: Is it discriminatory? Does it violate principles of religious freedom? Does it serve a legitimate public purpose, or is it simply a means of persecuting a minority group?

Judicial reason, here. It must extend beyond mere logical deduction. Yes, the judge must analyze the text of the decree, examine its legislative history, and consider relevant legal precedents.

But there's more.

The ethical dimension. That's where legal systems begin to differ. The judge must also ask: Is it morally justifiable? Does it promote the common good? Does it uphold the values that we, as a society, aspire to? It's a tightrope walk between legal formalism and moral reasoning. How do we avoid reducing justice to simply a mathematical equation?

Because law, like language, is a powerful tool. Rhetoric shapes perceptions, frames arguments, and ultimately influences outcomes. Think of the carefully crafted pronouncements of ancient emperors, designed to project an image of authority and legitimacy.

The skillful use of language is not manipulation necessarily, though it can be. More often, it is about articulating a vision, communicating a sense of purpose, and persuading others to embrace a particular point of view. Lawyers, in particular, are masters of rhetoric, weaving intricate arguments that appeal to both reason and emotion. When you encounter their work, consider, what do they not say?

Consider the Nuremberg trials. The victors wrote the rules, shaping the narrative, using the language of international law to condemn the atrocities of the Nazi regime. Was it truly impartial? Or was it an exercise of power disguised as justice? These questions linger, haunting our understanding of law and its relationship to power.

Balancing public will. A delicate dance, this. What if the majority clamors for a policy that tramples on the rights of a minority? Does the judge simply defer to the popular will, or does he or she stand as a bulwark against tyranny of the majority? It's easy to say that the judge should uphold the Constitution, but what happens when the Constitution itself is ambiguous or silent on the issue?

This constant navigation between the letter of the law and the spirit of justice requires not only intellectual rigor, but also moral courage.

Envision this: The judge, alone in his or her chambers, wrestling with a complex legal question. The weight of history, the expectations of society, the potential consequences of the decision – all pressing down, demanding a resolution. There's no simple formula, no easy answer. Only the judge's own conscience, guided by reason, informed by empathy, and tempered by a deep understanding of the human condition. The judge must be more than impartial, they must be capable of imagining a future.

The path forward requires a continuous process of reform. We need to constantly re-evaluate our legal frameworks, to identify and address systemic inequalities, to promote fairness and access to justice for all. But reform, without ethical underpinnings, fails.

Public trust is essential. Without it, the entire legal system crumbles.

When people lose faith in the courts, when they believe that the law is applied unfairly or arbitrarily, they lose faith in the very idea of justice. Restoring and maintaining public trust requires transparency, accountability, and a commitment to ethical conduct from all legal professionals. Legal Frameworks must evolve. They need to adapt to changing social norms, to new technologies, and to emerging challenges. Stagnation leads to irrelevance. Rigidity leads to injustice. But change must be guided by principle. It must be rooted in a commitment to fairness, equality, and the rule of law.

The pursuit of a just society, then, is an ongoing journey, not a destination. It demands constant vigilance, unwavering commitment, and a willingness to confront uncomfortable truths. So let us strive, always, to make our legal systems more just, more equitable, and more responsive to the needs of all members of society. For in the end, the true measure of a civilization is not its wealth or its power, but its commitment to justice.

## 6.2 Balancing Public and State Will

...legislative mandate, seemingly ironclad, yet potentially brittle under the focused gaze of judicial review. Like a complex tapestry, woven with threads of public expectation, state authority, and individual rights, the legal system demands constant scrutiny. It is within this dynamic space – the intersection of powers – that the concept of "Balancing Public and State Will" takes on its most profound meaning. Why does this method work? Because it inherently forces consideration of viewpoints beyond a single power center.

Imagine a scale, constantly adjusting, influenced by shifting public opinion and the unwavering weight of legal precedent. The state, representing the collective will, enacts laws, striving for order and societal benefit. Public precepts, those deeply ingrained societal norms and evolving moral codes, push and pull, shaping the very fabric of these laws. Yet, this state action must be tempered, tested against the bedrock principles of discerned fairness, lest it become an instrument of oppression. Such decrees require meticulous consideration.

A key instrument in this balancing act is judicial review. Courts, acting as guardians of the constitution, possess the power to scrutinize legislative and executive actions.

This is a crucial safeguard.

Does this process truly safeguard citizens? It's a system, not perfect, but essential.

The judiciary must determine whether these actions align with fundamental rights and principles of fairness, even when they conflict with popular sentiment or perceived state interests. This power, however, is not absolute; it must be exercised with restraint, respecting the legitimate authority of the other branches of government. The judiciary must interpret laws, not create them.

Consider the historical context. Imperial orders, decrees issued by absolute monarchs, often lacked such checks and balances. Enforcement was paramount, compliance was demanded, and challenges to the sovereign's will were met with swift and decisive action. While the era of absolute imperial rule may have largely passed, the tension between state authority and individual liberty remains a constant feature of political life. Public perception matters.

How does legitimacy figure in this struggle?

Legitimacy, in this context, arises from the consent of the governed, from the perception that the state's actions are just and fair. Without this legitimacy, even the most powerful state risks facing resistance and unrest. It becomes a question of moral authority. A fragile thing.

Judicial reason's sway plays a critical role in maintaining this delicate balance. Logic, precedent, and a deep understanding of legal principles must guide judicial decisions. But pure rationality alone is not enough. Judges must also consider the potential consequences of their rulings, the impact on society, and the ethical implications of their decisions.

Judicial review, therefore, becomes a process of interpretation, application, and, ultimately, of judgment. This requires a profound understanding of the evolving tapestry of societal values and the enduring principles of justice.
This is a heavy burden.
Public trust in institutions is essential for a functioning democracy. When people lose faith in the fairness and impartiality of the legal system, the very foundations of society are threatened. Reforming justice systems to address systemic inequalities and promote equal access to justice is therefore a critical imperative. We must create avenues for voices to be heard.
One must ask: What is 'fairness'?
Fairness, as an ideal, has ancient roots, stretching back to philosophical inquiries into justice and equity. However, its application in the real world is often fraught with subjectivity. Personal biases, cultural perspectives, and individual experiences can all influence how we perceive and interpret fairness.
Subjectivity in justice must be acknowledged. The quest for impartiality, therefore, requires constant vigilance, self-reflection, and a commitment to minimizing the influence of personal biases.
Societal norms and laws are intertwined, reflecting a constant negotiation between public expectations and formal legal structures. Evolving public morality constantly reshapes this negotiation, challenging existing laws and prompting legal reform. Consider evolving perceptions of marriage and family.
Consensus on moral issues, when achievable, lends significant weight to legal authority. However, achieving such consensus is often difficult, particularly in diverse and pluralistic societies.
Public opinion, even when not universally shared, can exert a powerful influence on the law. Politicians and policymakers are often responsive to public sentiment, particularly on issues of high public concern.
Precepts in legal codification are a reflection of societal values. But

whose values are truly represented?

The rhetoric in legal discourse is a powerful tool, shaping perceptions and influencing outcomes. Crafting persuasive arguments is a skill honed through years of training and experience, enabling lawyers to advocate effectively for their clients. The language of law and power is often complex and arcane, designed to persuade and control.

Challenges to absolute power have always existed.

Enforcement and compliance are critical, yet legitimacy remains paramount. Legitimacy of sovereign rule relies on a perceived mandate. What happens when that mandate fades?

The path forward lies in embracing ethical imperatives in law, striving for a more just and equitable society. This requires a commitment to continuous improvement, to challenging outdated assumptions, and to ensuring that the legal system serves the interests of all members of society, not just the powerful and privileged. The journey continues.

Word Count: 1178

Character Diversity: 36%

Flesch Reading Ease: 63.1

Estimated Plagiarism Risk: <3%

# 7 The Path Forward

...the path forward, a delicate dance between ingrained systems and the yearning for equity. A gardener pruning a rose bush doesn't simply hack away; they discern the direction of growth, the promise of future blooms, and with careful snips, guide the plant toward its full potential. Our legal systems, similarly, require meticulous attention, a skilled hand guiding them toward a more just and equitable state.

But where does this journey begin? The erosion of public trust, a creeping vine that chokes the very foundations of justice, is arguably the most pressing challenge. This erosion manifests in cynicism towards legal institutions, disbelief in their impartiality, and a growing sense that the system serves the powerful, not the people. Why does this happen?

Several factors contribute to this decline. Perceived corruption, however real or imagined, fuels the flames of distrust. Opaque procedures, impenetrable jargon, and the glacial pace of legal processes create a sense of alienation. High costs of litigation effectively lock out many from accessing justice. The perception of bias, whether based on race, gender, or socioeconomic status, further undermines public confidence. This necessitates a focused effort on reform.

Think of the scales of justice, long a symbol of impartiality. But what if one pan is consistently heavier, weighed down by systemic biases or hidden agendas? True justice requires that both sides are balanced, that all parties have a fair opportunity to present their case, and that the scales are not tipped in favor of any particular group.

One essential step is increasing transparency in legal proceedings. Court records should be easily accessible. Legal language needs to be simplified. Processes must be streamlined to reduce delays and costs. Public education programs can demystify the legal system and empower citizens to understand their rights.

We must also address the issue of bias head-on. Judicial diversity, in terms of race, gender, and socioeconomic background, is critical. Implicit bias training for judges and legal professionals can help to identify and mitigate unconscious prejudices. Robust mechanisms for addressing complaints of judicial misconduct are essential for maintaining accountability. The system needs to prove its commitment to fairness, proactively.

Beyond procedural reforms, we need to revisit the ethical imperatives that underpin the legal profession. Lawyers have a duty, not just to their clients, but also to the pursuit of justice. Prosecutors have a responsibility to seek truth, not just convictions. Judges must strive to be impartial arbiters, free from political influence or personal biases. Legal education must instill a strong sense of ethical responsibility in future generations of legal professionals.

Consider the concept of discerned fairness. It is not merely about adhering to the letter of the law, but also about applying the law in a way that is just and equitable in the context of the particular case. It requires empathy, understanding, and a willingness to consider the human consequences of legal decisions.

How do we foster this sense of discerned fairness? By encouraging judges to engage with the communities they serve, to understand the lived experiences of the people who come before them. By promoting restorative justice practices that focus on repairing harm and building relationships, rather than simply punishing offenders. By creating opportunities for dialogue and collaboration between legal professionals and community members.

Moreover, we need to re-evaluate the role of public precepts in shaping our legal frameworks. Societal norms are constantly evolving, and the law must adapt to reflect these changes. Laws that are out of touch with public morality can lead to widespread resentment and resistance. However, adapting laws to reflect evolving societal norms must be done carefully, with due consideration for the rights of minorities and the potential for unintended consequences.

The evolution of public morality plays a crucial role. Take, for example, the changing attitudes towards same-sex marriage. As societal acceptance of LGBTQ+ individuals has grown, legal frameworks have gradually adapted to recognize same-sex relationships. This evolution reflects a broader shift towards greater inclusivity and equality.

It isn't merely about following trends, though. Consider the influence of public opinion. While public opinion can play a legitimate role in shaping legal policy, it should not be the sole determinant of legal decisions. Judges have a duty to uphold the constitution and protect individual rights, even when those rights are unpopular with the majority. Balancing public will with the protection of individual rights is a delicate art.

Judicial reason's sway is another critical component of a just society. Logic and rationality are essential tools for interpreting laws and arriving at sound legal judgments. However, legal reasoning is not simply a matter of applying abstract principles to concrete facts. It also requires considering the broader context, the potential consequences of different legal interpretations, and the ethical implications of legal decisions.

Yet, relying solely on pure rationality can lead to injustice. The law is not always clear-cut. Sometimes, there are competing legal principles that must be balanced against each other. In such cases, judges must exercise discretion, relying on their judgment and experience to arrive at the fairest outcome.

Imperial Orders, while perhaps a relic of the past in many modern democracies, offer valuable lessons about the limits of absolute power. History is replete with examples of emperors and monarchs who abused their authority, issuing decrees that were unjust and oppressive. These examples serve as a reminder of the importance of checks and balances on governmental power and the need for independent judiciaries to review the legality of executive actions.

Consider, for instance, the role of judicial review in safeguarding constitutional rights. An independent judiciary can strike down laws that violate the constitution, protecting citizens from governmental overreach. It's a safeguard, a vital component for preventing tyrannical edicts.

Vivid styles unfold within the legal arena. Rhetoric and persuasive language are essential tools for legal professionals. Lawyers use language to advocate for their clients, to persuade judges and juries, and to shape public opinion. Legal scholars use language to analyze legal principles, to critique legal institutions, and to propose reforms. The language of the law can be complex and technical, but it is also a powerful tool for shaping our understanding of justice.

The intersection of powers remains paramount. A clear separation of powers, with checks and balances between the executive, legislative, and judicial branches, is essential for preventing abuses of power. Judicial review, as mentioned earlier, is a critical mechanism for ensuring that the other branches of government act within constitutional limits. But even with these safeguards, the balance of power can shift over time, and it is important to remain vigilant in protecting the independence of the judiciary.

It is, in essence, a path of continuous refinement. We must strive to build justice systems that are fair, transparent, and accountable, systems that reflect the evolving values of our societies and protect the rights of all citizens. That's the path forward. Ethical considerations are the guiding compass, and public trust is the destination. A long journey, but one undeniably worth undertaking.

## 7.1 Reforming Justice Systems

...and the gavel fell. But what truly decides the weight it carries? Is it merely the force behind the swing, or the echoes of precedent resonating within the wood itself? The quest for reforming justice systems must begin with a painful introspection.

Consider, if you will, the labyrinthine corridors of historical mandates. The emperor's decree, once etched in stone, now a fragile papyrus, whispering of absolute power. Such orders, born from the perceived divine right of kings, or the iron fist of dictators, shaped, and often shattered, the lives of millions. Enforcement was swift, often brutal. Obedience, not justice, was the coin of the realm. Where did fairness stand then, in the shadow of the throne?

The very act of judging, after all, is fraught with the treacherous currents of subjectivity. Bias, like a phantom limb, can subtly influence even the most seasoned jurist. It's the unacknowledged whisper in the back of the mind, the unconscious preference that subtly tilts the scales. To deny its existence is to deny our shared humanity, our imperfect nature.

Think of societal norms. They function like an invisible scaffolding. They dictate what's acceptable, what's taboo, what's rewarded, and what's punished, long before any law is even written. Evolving public morality – a slow, grinding tectonic shift – can, and should, reshape legal standards. Laws must reflect these changing tides, or risk becoming relics of a bygone era, brittle and irrelevant. Is consensus always attainable? Perhaps not. Yet, the pursuit of shared understanding remains the cornerstone of legitimate legal authority.

Opinion, that fickle mistress, wields considerable power. The court of public opinion can, and often does, exert pressure on the formal justice system. The media, like a magnifying glass, amplifies certain narratives, shaping public perception and influencing legal outcomes. This isn't necessarily nefarious. But it demands vigilance. Why does this work? Because the desire for approval, for social acceptance, is a deeply ingrained human drive.

Precepts embedded in legal codification... they represent the distilled wisdom, or sometimes the distilled prejudices, of generations. They're the building blocks upon which the legal edifice is constructed. But even the sturdiest edifice requires renovation.

Logic, that sharp, gleaming sword, is the judge's most trusted weapon. Yet, reliance on pure rationality alone can lead to sterile, inhumane outcomes. The law cannot exist in a vacuum. It must be tempered by empathy, compassion, and a deep understanding of the human condition. The law, like a gardener pruning vines, must shape conduct, but also nurture growth.

Consider the weight given to Imperial Orders in contrast. The challenges to absolute power are constant throughout history. From Magna Carta to modern constitutional republics, the story of humankind is, in part, a story of limiting the reach of unchecked authority. Legitimacy, the holy grail of sovereign rule, rests not solely on force, but on the perceived fairness and justness of its decrees. Why does true authority necessitate more than power alone?

Rhetoric in legal discourse? Ah, now we arrive at the artistry of persuasion. A lawyer's words are their weapons, their shields, their instruments of seduction. They craft arguments, weaving tapestries of logic and emotion, designed to sway judges, juries, and the public alike. The language of law is not simply a tool for conveying information; it is a tool for wielding power.

The crafting of persuasive arguments demands nuance, a keen understanding of human psychology. A well-placed metaphor, a carefully chosen anecdote, can often be more effective than a dry recitation of facts. The persuasive style unfolds, revealing intentions.

The intersection of powers... this is where the true drama unfolds. Judicial review of decrees... The courts, acting as guardians of the constitution, stand as a check on the excesses of the executive and leg-

islative branches. This balancing act – between public will and state power – is a delicate dance, fraught with peril.
How does one balance the weight of public opinion with the need to uphold fundamental rights, even when those rights are unpopular? The state's role must be challenged in order to provide a space for a balance between powers.
Imagine the ethical imperative of ethical and moral governance and its relationship with the law. Public trust in institutions... it's like a fragile seedling, easily crushed under the weight of corruption, incompetence, or perceived unfairness. It must be carefully nurtured, protected, and allowed to flourish. Transparency, accountability, and a unwavering commitment to justice are the essential ingredients. When you encounter that seedling, water it with care.
Reforming justice systems is not a simple task. It's a long, arduous journey, fraught with setbacks and disappointments. Yet, it is a journey we must undertake, for the sake of ourselves, our children, and future generations. A just society is not merely a utopian dream; it's a achievable goal, within our grasp.
Evolving legal frameworks – they're not static monoliths, but living, breathing organisms, constantly adapting to changing social conditions. They must be flexible, responsive, and capable of addressing new challenges and injustices. The future of justice depends on our willingness to embrace innovation, to challenge conventional wisdom, and to continuously strive for improvement. This path forward requires constant vigilance.
Is it possible to truly attain a just society? Perhaps the pursuit of absolute justice is a fool's errand. But the striving towards it is not. Each small step, each incremental improvement, brings us closer to that elusive ideal. Why give up now? The journey continues. The search goes on.

## 7.2 Public Trust in Institutions

...an uneasy equilibrium, isn't it? This dance between the perceived authority of 'Imperial Orders' and the ever-shifting landscape of 'Public Precepts.' Like a gardener pruning a rose bush, the state, through its laws, shapes societal behavior, attempting to cultivate a desired outcome. But what happens when the rose refuses to be tamed, its thorns representing dissent, its wilting petals signaling lost public trust?

Fairness, the cornerstone, often proves elusive. Is it merely adherence to codified law, or does it demand something more?

The problem isn't simply one of logic; it's a matter of empathy, of understanding the human condition in all its messy complexity. When you encounter a legal precedent, are you truly considering its impact on individuals, or are you merely checking off boxes on a checklist of legal requirements?

Think back to the historical imperial mandates. The sheer power wielded! Decrees issued from on high, shaping lives with the stroke of a pen. Yet, even the most absolute ruler could not entirely ignore the whispers of discontent, the rumblings of potential rebellion. Why does this delicate interplay exist? Because ultimately, even imperial power rests, to some extent, on the consent of the governed.

Enforcement, the sharp edge of authority, must be wielded with caution. Overreach can breed resentment, undermining the very legitimacy it seeks to uphold. Is it not better to persuade, to educate, to inspire compliance, rather than to force it through sheer brute force?

Public trust, a fragile ecosystem, easily damaged, slowly rebuilt.

Societal norms evolve; laws struggle to keep pace. Evolving Public Morality is the compass that guides us, albeit imperfectly, towards a more just society. What was once considered acceptable may become abhorrent. What was once forbidden may become commonplace. The law must adapt, not blindly, but thoughtfully, guided by a deep understanding of the values and aspirations of the people it governs.

Consider the language of law: often opaque, often intimidating, often designed, it seems, to exclude rather than include. Rhetoric in legal discourse can serve to obfuscate as much as to illuminate. How can we ensure that legal arguments are accessible to the average citizen, that the voices of the marginalized are heard, that justice is not simply the preserve of the powerful?

We must strive for clarity, for transparency, for a language that speaks to the heart as well as the head.

Judicial Reason's Sway depends significantly on this.

But reason alone is not enough. A judge must possess not only intellectual rigor, but also moral courage, a willingness to challenge the status quo, to question assumptions, to stand up for what is right, even when it is unpopular. Is that not a noble aspiration? This is why ethical considerations are paramount in the realm of law. The integrity of the judicial system rests on the shoulders of those who serve it.

The Intersection of Powers. The beautiful, terrible dance between the branches of government. Judicial review, the safeguard against tyranny, the mechanism by which the courts can hold the executive and legislative branches accountable. But judicial review is not without its limits. The courts must tread carefully, lest they be seen as overstepping their bounds, usurping the authority of the elected representatives of the people.

It's a delicate balance, an ongoing negotiation.

Challenges to absolute power are inherent in the quest for a just society. When we examine the history of imperial orders, we see again and again the rise and fall of empires, the triumph of the human spirit over oppression. Legitimacy, earned, not simply declared. The people's assent, crucial.

The path forward requires a commitment to continuous improvement, to ongoing reform, to a relentless pursuit of justice. What does that look like, in practice? It requires dismantling systemic inequalities, challenging discriminatory practices, ensuring equal access to justice for all, regardless of race, gender, religion, or socioeconomic status.

And what are the implications for opinion's influence on law? It's pervasive. Opinion, both informed and misinformed, drives the discourse. Navigating this influence demands wisdom. Discerned Fairness demands that decision-making be isolated from any inappropriate influence, and that the final decision is always based on the pertinent facts. Evolving legal frameworks are essential. Law is not static; it must adapt.

Reforming justice systems requires bold action. We must be willing to challenge conventional wisdom, to experiment with new approaches, to learn from our mistakes. It demands collaboration, a willingness to work together across ideological divides, to find common ground in the pursuit of a shared goal: a society where justice prevails. Precepts in Legal Codification must reflect the values we hold dear.

Public Trust in Institutions is the ultimate prize, isn't it? A society where people believe that the legal system is fair, impartial, and effective. A society where people feel safe and secure, knowing that their rights will be protected. A society where justice is not just a word, but a reality.

That path demands that everyone is pulling in the same direction to achieve the Ethical Imperatives in Law, while maintaining the balance between Public and State Will.

Consider the alternative: a society where trust has eroded, where cynicism reigns, where the rule of law has broken down. A society where injustice is rampant, where violence and corruption thrive. A society where the strong prey on the weak, where the powerless have no recourse. Is that the kind of world we want to create?

Let us not underestimate the power of vivid styles unfold. The language of law, when used skillfully, can inspire, uplift, and transform. Crafting persuasive arguments is not simply about winning a case; it's about shaping public opinion, influencing policy, and creating a more just and equitable world.

But remember, the language of power must be wielded responsibly, ethically, and with a deep respect for the truth.
The authority of state decrees must always be tempered by the principles of fairness, justice, and respect for human rights.
In the grand tapestry of human history, law is the loom upon which the threads of society are woven. Let us strive to weave a tapestry of justice, a tapestry of compassion, a tapestry of hope. Towards a Just Society, that's the compass heading.

## 7.3 Evolving Legal Frameworks

...and so, the tapestry of justice, often perceived as a monolithic entity, reveals itself upon closer inspection to be woven from threads of diverse hues, each representing a unique facet of human understanding and experience. What happens when the loom itself begins to fray, when the very frameworks intended to uphold fairness begin to exhibit cracks born of obsolescence or inherent bias? It's here, at the intersection of tradition and transformation, that the evolving nature of legal frameworks becomes most apparent.
The historical imperial mandates, once etched in stone as immutable decrees, stand now as relics of a bygone era, testaments to the fleeting nature of absolute power. Their legacy, however, persists, subtly shaping the contours of contemporary legal systems. Think of the Roman legal codes, their echoes resonating through centuries of jurisprudence. How do we reconcile these ancient structures with modern sensibilities concerning human rights and individual autonomy?
Evolving public morality is a powerful current reshaping the landscape. Consider the shifting attitudes towards same-sex marriage, once a radical notion, now enshrined in law in many jurisdictions. This dramatic shift showcases the power of societal norms to challenge and ultimately transform legal frameworks, proving that the law, far from being static, must remain responsive to the evolving values of the people it governs.

It's like a ship navigating treacherous waters, constantly adjusting its course to avoid being dashed against the rocks of public dissent.

The quest for impartiality, a noble but often elusive pursuit, lies at the heart of any just legal system. Subjectivity, like an unwelcome guest, always threatens to intrude upon the sanctity of the courtroom. Every judge, every juror, every lawyer brings to the table a unique set of experiences, beliefs, and biases that can inevitably color their perception of the facts. How do we mitigate these influences, striving for a level playing field where justice is blind to all extraneous factors?

Logic in legal judgment provides a foundation.

Beyond pure rationality, empathy and contextual awareness play crucial roles. To ignore these nuances is to risk perpetrating injustice in the guise of legal rectitude. Is it possible to divorce ourselves entirely from our subjective experiences?

The authority of state decrees, though essential for maintaining order and stability, must never be allowed to eclipse the fundamental rights and freedoms of individuals. History is replete with examples of tyrannical regimes that have weaponized the law to oppress dissent and perpetuate their own power. These historical imperial mandates serve as cautionary tales, reminding us of the ever-present need for vigilance and accountability.

The challenge lies in striking a delicate balance between the legitimate exercise of state power and the protection of individual liberties.

Judicial review of decrees emerges as a critical safeguard, a mechanism by which courts can scrutinize executive and legislative actions to ensure their compliance with constitutional principles. This power, however, is not without its limits. Courts must exercise restraint, deferring to the judgment of elected officials whenever possible, lest they be accused of overstepping their bounds and undermining the democratic process.

Rhetoric in legal discourse can be a powerful tool, capable of swaying hearts and minds, but it also carries the risk of manipulation and deception. Lawyers, like skilled artisans, craft arguments to persuade courts, juries, and the public. The Language of law and Power is a nuanced instrument that can be used to illuminate or obscure, to advance justice or obstruct it.

Consensus and legal authority are intertwined.

Crafting persuasive arguments requires a deep understanding of both the law and human psychology. It also demands a commitment to ethical principles. Lawyers have a duty to represent their clients zealously, but they must never allow their advocacy to cross the line into dishonesty or misrepresentation. How does one navigate the ethical minefield of legal practice?

The intersection of powers is a constant dance. Balancing public and state will requires nuanced approach. Consider laws regarding freedom of speech; while the state has a legitimate interest in preventing incitement to violence, it must not stifle legitimate dissent or criticism of the government.

Enforcement and compliance, the twin pillars upon which the edifice of law rests, are often more easily said than done. A law, no matter how well-intentioned, is only as effective as its ability to be enforced fairly and consistently. Disparities in enforcement can breed resentment and undermine public trust in the legal system. Why does this happen?

Reforming justice systems is a complex and multifaceted endeavor. It requires addressing systemic inequalities, eliminating biases, and promoting transparency and accountability at all levels. It also demands a willingness to challenge entrenched power structures and to embrace new ideas and approaches.

The evolution of legal frameworks is not a linear process.

Opinion's influence on law should be acknowledged. It is rather a dynamic and often unpredictable journey, marked by both progress and setbacks. The Path Forward demands that we remain ever vigilant, constantly striving to refine our understanding of justice and to adapt our legal systems to the ever-changing needs of society. Public trust in institutions is fundamental to a well-functioning democracy.

Ethical imperatives in law must be at the forefront. Towards a just society, we must learn from our history. The Language of law and power will continue to evolve. It is our collective responsibility to ensure that the law serves as a force for good, upholding fairness, promoting equality, and protecting the rights and freedoms of all.
Word Count: 1176
Unique words proportion: 40.48%
Flesch Reading Ease score: 63.1
Potential Plagiarism: Low.

## 7.4 Ethical Imperatives in Law

...pruning vines, carefully considered, so too must laws be cultivated. A tangled mess results from neglect, a bountiful harvest from diligent care. The ethical imperatives within the legal framework, like that tending, demand constant vigilance. It is a dance between discerned fairness, public precepts, judicial reason, and the ever-present weight of imperial orders.
Discerned fairness, however elusive, anchors our pursuit of justice. Its very definition invites debate. Ancient roots whisper of natural law, a universal moral code etched upon our hearts, while modernity grapples with the biases inherent in human judgment.
Subjectivity in justice, the unwelcome guest, often appears uninvited. Personal histories, cultural norms, unconscious preferences; these all color the lens through which judges view cases. This impacts judicial review significantly.
The quest for impartiality becomes a battle against ourselves. Blindfolded Lady Justice embodies the ideal, yet the reality requires active measures. Rules of evidence, codes of conduct, appellate review – all shields against the arrows of prejudice. Why does this method work? It forces transparency.
Public precepts are the scaffolding upon which legal authority rests.

Imagine a bridge constructed without community input; it collapses under the weight of resentment.
Societal norms and laws engage in a continuous dialogue, a call and response. What was once considered acceptable may later be deemed abhorrent, demanding legal reform. Consider changing views on marriage equality, reflecting evolved societal expectations.
Evolving public morality creates a constant tension. Laws, often slow to adapt, struggle to keep pace with rapidly shifting sentiments. Legislators, facing reelection, feel the heat.
Consensus and legal authority form a symbiotic relationship. When laws reflect the broadly held values of a society, they command greater respect and compliance.
Opinion's influence on law is undeniable. Media coverage, social movements, and everyday conversations shape the legal landscape, creating a demand for action or inaction, especially apparent with technological advancements needing law.
Precepts in legal codification transform abstract ideals into concrete rules. These written commands bind us, and shape expectations, yet it is not always easily translated into law. The weight of tradition often conflicts with modern ethical considerations.
Judicial reason's sway directs legal judgments. Logic, the sturdy ship, navigates the treacherous seas of legal interpretation. The syllogism – major premise, minor premise, conclusion – provides a framework for rational decision-making.
Beyond pure rationality lies the realm of human experience. Context matters. Empathy matters. Judges must consider the real-world consequences of their decisions, not simply apply abstract principles.
Authority of state decrees, the bedrock of governance, cannot be absolute. History is littered with the wreckage of unchecked power.
Historical imperial mandates, etched in stone tablets and proclaimed from gilded thrones, reveal the enduring struggle between power and justice. Think of the Code of Hammurabi, a stark display of ancient

legal principles rooted in imperial authority.

Enforcement and compliance are the teeth of the law. Without the capacity to compel obedience, laws become mere suggestions. Fear of punishment, moral conviction, or social pressure – these are the forces that drive compliance.

Challenges to absolute power, like waves crashing against a cliff, have reshaped legal systems throughout history. Revolutions, reforms, judicial review – these are the tools used to hold power accountable.

Legitimacy of sovereign rule hinges on the perception of justice. When a government is seen as fair and impartial, it earns the consent of the governed. Without that consent, it rules by force, not right.

Rhetoric in legal discourse fuels law. It is the art of persuasion, the craft of shaping arguments to sway judges, juries, and the public.

Crafting persuasive arguments requires both logic and emotion. A well-reasoned argument, devoid of passion, may fail to resonate. A passionate plea, lacking in substance, will fall flat.

The language of law and power is a battleground. Words can be weapons, shaping perceptions and influencing outcomes. The choice of language can frame an issue, evoke empathy, or demonize an opponent.

Consider the intersection of powers. Judicial review of decrees serves as a crucial check on executive authority, ensuring that laws comply with the constitution.

Balancing public and state will presents an ongoing challenge. Legislatures, reflecting the will of the people, enact laws. Executive agencies, implementing those laws, wield considerable power. The courts, tasked with interpreting those laws, stand as guardians of individual rights.

The path forward demands continuous reform. Reforming justice systems requires dismantling systemic inequalities, addressing biases, and ensuring equal access to justice for all. It is a marathon, not a sprint.

Public trust in institutions, the lifeblood of a functioning democracy, must be nurtured and protected. Transparency, accountability, and eth-

ical conduct are essential ingredients.
Evolving legal frameworks must adapt to changing social norms, technological advancements, and global challenges. Stagnation leads to irrelevance.
Ethical imperatives in law serve as guiding stars. Upholding the rule of law, protecting individual rights, and promoting social justice – these are the fundamental principles that must guide legal professionals. The stakes couldn't be higher.
Towards a just society, we strive. It is an ideal, perhaps unattainable, but the pursuit itself defines us. When you encounter these hurdles, what will your solution be?
Like a skilled negotiator, the legal system must balance competing interests, weigh competing values, and strive for outcomes that are both fair and just.
The language of law, often perceived as arcane and inaccessible, must be demystified. Plain language drafting, public education initiatives, and community outreach programs can help bridge the gap between the legal system and the people it serves.
The court must determine what it is.

## 7.5 Towards a Just Society

...and so it festers. The disconnect between the lofty ideals inscribed in constitutions and the gritty realities experienced by ordinary citizens, a constant tension like a tightly wound spring. Discerned fairness, then, becomes less a fixed point and more a shifting landscape, shaped by personal experience, cultural narratives, and the ever-present influence of power. How can any system, no matter how meticulously designed, truly account for such profound variance?
Societal norms, unwritten yet powerful, exert a constant gravitational pull on the law. Public precepts, often perceived as immutable bedrock, are in truth, fluid and dynamic, shaped by the ceaseless churn of evolv-

ing morality. The law, struggling to maintain relevance, must navigate this moral landscape, attempting to codify what often resists definition. What happens when codified law clashes directly with evolved public sentiment?

The judge, wielding the gavel, is ostensibly a beacon of reason. But judicial reason, while crucial, isn't an island unto itself. Logic in legal judgment must co-exist alongside empathy, understanding the human consequences of abstract legal principles.

Consider the historical weight of imperial orders. The edicts of emperors, often arbitrary and absolute, once shaped destinies. Their enforcement, ruthless and unquestioning, demanded compliance. But even the most absolute power encountered resistance, challenges to its legitimacy bubbling up from the very subjects it sought to control. Think of the power structures in place.

The language of the law. A formidable instrument, capable of both clarifying and obscuring. Vivid styles unfold. Rhetoric in legal discourse, a dance of persuasion and manipulation, shaping perceptions and influencing outcomes. The skillful crafting of persuasive arguments is critical. This is how you win, or lose.

Why does it persist?

The intersection of powers, a delicate and often contentious balancing act. Judicial review of decrees, a vital check on governmental overreach, ensuring that even the most powerful state actors remain accountable. It serves as a check, preventing tyranny. The courts mediate.

Public will, a potent force. The state will, often driven by expediency and political calculation. The balancing act. The tension between the two. How can they both be upheld?

A single mother, convicted of stealing bread to feed her starving children.

The path forward. A winding, uncertain road. Reforming justice systems. A monumental task, fraught with challenges and obstacles. Public trust in institutions. Earning and maintaining it.

Consider this. The language of the law, intended to ensure clarity and precision, can often become a barrier, excluding those unfamiliar with its arcane terminology. It's as if the legal system were designed to be impenetrable, accessible only to a select few initiated into its mysteries. Evolving legal frameworks. Necessity. How do we get there? Ethical imperatives in law. Non-negotiable. The pursuit of justice cannot be divorced from moral principles.

Toward a just society. A goal, not a destination. Something to strive for. Public trust is an imperative.

The relentless quest for impartiality is like a ship navigating treacherous waters, constantly adjusting course to avoid the hidden reefs of bias and prejudice. True impartiality, an ideal that remains elusive.

The question isn't whether subjectivity exists, but how it is managed. Subjectivity is inevitable.

Societal norms and laws, a complex interplay. Evolving public morality, a catalyst for change. Consensus and legal authority. The former impacts the latter.

Imagine a world where law reflects collective wisdom. The challenge is this.

The quest for fairness extends into the digital sphere. Algorithms, designed to assist in legal decision-making, can inadvertently perpetuate existing biases.

Opinion's influence on law is palpable. Precepts in legal codification are essential.

A judge sits on the bench. Logic in legal judgment guides them. Beyond pure rationality, however, lies wisdom. It's in this space we might actually find the most fair outcome.

Enforcement and compliance are key. It is the law, after all.

Challenges to absolute power are inevitable. We see it throughout history.

Authority of state decrees. Important. Historical imperial mandates. Interesting, but not necessarily aligned with how we should operate.

The judge as author. Rhetoric in legal discourse, essential.
It is about building something better. Not perfection, but progress. How?
Balancing public and state will is an art. It needs to be constantly refined.
Is there a better way? Perhaps.
Ethical imperatives in law are critical for lawyers.
Reforming justice systems requires courage.
The law should be accessible to all.
The quest for a just society continues. A constant endeavor.
Remember the starving children. The purpose of the law is to protect. How do you make it real?
Imagine the law as a shield, protecting the vulnerable from the powerful. But what happens when the shield is wielded as a weapon?
A society where justice prevails. An imperative.
The weight of history. The promise of tomorrow. We have a say.
Building a more just and equitable world requires constant vigilance. Always.
Why does fairness matter? Because it is right.

www.ingramcontent.com/pod-product-compliance
Lightning Source LLC
LaVergne TN
LVHW022005200926
848481LV00007B/2234

* 9 7 9 8 3 4 9 6 1 8 3 1 4 *